W9-AYV-650

TALENT
MAGNET

Other Titles by Mark Miller:

The High-Performance Series

Chess Not Checkers

Leaders Made Here

Other Books

The Heart of Leadership

The Secret of Teams

Coauthored with Ken Blanchard

Great Leaders Grow

The Secret

Field Guides

The Heart of Leadership

The Secret of Teams

Field Guides coauthored with Randy Gravitt

The Secret

Leaders Made Here

Chess Not Checkers

TALENT MAGNET

HOW TO ATTRACT AND
KEEP THE BEST PEOPLE

MARK MILLER

Bestselling author of *Leaders Made Here*
and *Chess Not Checkers*

BK

Berrett–Koehler Publishers, Inc.
a BK Business book

Berrett-Koehler Publishers, Inc.
1333 Broadway, Suite 1000
Oakland, CA 94612-1921
Tel: (510) 817-2277   Fax: (510) 817-2278   www.bkconnection.com

Ordering Information
Quantity sales. Special discounts are available on quantity purchases by corporations, associations, and others. For details, contact the "Special Sales Department" at the Berrett-Koehler address above.

Individual sales. Berrett-Koehler publications are available through most bookstores. They can also be ordered directly from Berrett-Koehler: Tel: (800) 929-2929;
Fax: (802) 864-7626; www.bkconnection.com.

Orders for college textbook/course adoption use. Please contact Berrett-Koehler: Tel: (800) 929-2929; Fax: (802) 864-7626.

Distributed to the U.S. trade and internationally by Penguin Random House Publisher Services.

Berrett-Koehler and the BK logo are registered trademarks of Berrett-Koehler Publishers, Inc.

Printed in the United States of America

Berrett-Koehler booksare printed on long-lasting acid-free paper. When it is available, we choose paper that has been manufactured by environmentally responsible processes. These may include using trees grown in sustainable forests, incorporating recycled paper, minimizing chlorine in bleaching, or recycling the energy produced at the paper mill.

Production Management: Michael Bass Associates
Book designer: Julie Gallagher
Cover designer: Lindsay Miller

Library of Congress Cataloging-in-Publication Data
Names: Miller, Mark, 1959– author.
Title: Talent magnet : how to attract and keep the best people / Mark Miller.
Description: First Edition. | Oakland : Berrett-Koehler Publishers, 2018. |
    Series: The high performance ; 3
Identifiers: LCCN 2017050578 | ISBN 9781523094950 (hardback)
Subjects: LCSH: Employees—Recruiting. | Ability. | Success in business. |
    BISAC: BUSINESS & ECONOMICS / Leadership. | BUSINESS & ECONOMICS /
    Management.
Classification: LCC HF5549.5.R44 M55 2018 | DDC 658.3/111—dc23
LC record available at https://lccn.loc.gov/2017050578

First Edition
26 25 24 23 22 21 20 19 18   10 9 8 7 6 5 4 3 2

Dad, thanks for showing me how to live,
and most importantly, how to love.
Your influence will reverberate for generations!

Contents

Introduction

Increase the caliber of your players and you increase your chances of winning.

Because this principle is universally understood, finding and keeping the best people has become a preoccupation for many leaders. However, convincing talented people to join our organizations has only become more difficult in recent years.

Our never-ending quest for the most talented people has been made even more difficult by changing demographics, fluctuating employment statistics, increased competition, and shifting expectations. These forces have left many organizations with a critical shortfall of people. The effect: a virtual war for talent. The research, and the book you now hold were born in this context.

Given the growing need for talented people, my team wondered: *What is really required to attract "Top Talent?"*

What do you do when you have a question? You Google it. What do you do if Google doesn't know the answer? You either put your question in the "too hard pile" or find the answer for yourself. That's where we found ourselves. The answers at our disposal were somewhere between inadequate and nonexistent.

Our next step was to contact global thought leaders in the area of human resources—surely, they could tell us what attracts Top Talent. We were shocked time and time again after being told, "No one has done the research to answer your question."

Finally, with no credible answers readily available, we decided to commission the work ourselves.

After a ground-breaking, quantitative study focused specifically on what attracts Top Talent, combined with hundreds of face-to-face interviews with top performers and on-the-job ethnography, the chief insight, among many:

> ### *What attracts and keeps Top Talent is different from what attracts and keeps typical talent.*

This book will not only clarify these differences; it can serve as a mirror for you and your organization. Are you really offering what Top Talent wants? If not, why not? And, don't be surprised if, along the way, you are challenged regarding how you see your role as a leader.

The War for Talent

"How could this be happening?" Blake thought.

He had just walked out of a meeting with his Human Resources team. They had informed him they would not be able to staff the company's near-term plans and suggested to Blake he reduce the organization's growth goals. They could see no way to find enough qualified people to hit their targets. The shortfall was large—and growing.

His team explained the elements of a perfect storm—a mix of economic, demographic, and competitive pressures all coming to bear simultaneously. The result: they had been thrust into the 'war for talent.'

Blake was not used to this type of news. Since becoming the CEO, his early decision to build a high-performance organization had paid huge dividends. All the outcome metrics had continued to climb. This new information could change everything. Blake knew people were central to their success. Suddenly, over the course of one short meeting, people had now become his greatest point of vulnerability.

Although the recommendation of his team was unexpected, if Blake was *totally* honest with himself, the early warning signs of an impending storm had been in the air for months. A combination of his optimism, overdelegation, and busyness had prevented him from connecting the dots sooner.

A combination of his optimism, overdelegation, and busyness had prevented him from connecting the dots sooner.

As he reflected on what he had missed, he remembered losing several key people recently. More troubling, he recalled each of the top candidates for their replacements declined offers to join his organization. And, to make matters worse, he could also recall a few clues that their talent pipeline was looking more like a dripping faucet. For example, Blake wrote personal notes to new employees; he hadn't been asked to write as many in the previous months.

What Blake had once considered a Human Resources issue had now clearly become *his* issue. He couldn't help but wonder if perhaps he should have taken a bigger interest in this topic years ago.

● ● ●

As Blake walked to his car, his thoughts shifted to the dinner he was about to attend. It was a peer-mentoring group—eight CEOs from a diverse set of businesses.

Tonight would be their first meeting. Potential discussion topics had been submitted in advance to the moderator. As he drove to the event, he wondered what the group would address. He had submitted three potential topics; unfortunately, staffing was not one of them.

Over dinner, the attendees engaged in casual conversation and introductions. In addition to ethnic, gender, and age diversity, these leaders represented industries from totally different sectors: high tech, manufacturing, retail, hospitality, construction, education, healthcare, and even a global nonprofit organization.

As dessert was bring served, Martha Livingston called the group to order. "Welcome," she said with a warm, inviting smile. "Thanks for agreeing to be part of this experiment. My hypothesis is simple: we can learn from each other. Tonight is our first opportunity to see if I'm right or not.

"As we discussed previously via email, we will address one topic per meeting. The objective is to share what we're learning about a given issue. Tonight, based on an overwhelming level of interest, we're going to talk about how to find and keep talented people."

Blake breathed a sigh of relief.

Martha continued, "I'll kick off the conversation. I've been in business for forty-five years, and this may be the biggest talent mess I have ever seen. If we can't crack the code soon, we're going to have to slow our growth plans."

Bart Elkridge nodded his head and agreed. "I can get people," he said. "People aren't the problem. It's the caliber of people I worry about. Ours is a complicated business. Not just anyone can, or is willing, to do the hard work we require."

I can get people. People aren't the problem. It's the caliber of people I worry about.

One by one the attendees spoke, each addressing the problem but no one offering any solutions.

"Hi, I'm Blake. It's been energizing to hear from each of you. I'm the least experienced guy here. I've only been in my role about a decade, and I've never seen the talent challenge this bad. But, here's my view: The world is still full of talented men and women. Some of you referred to them as A players. They still want to work and are eager to contribute. Why don't we go get them?"

Martha responded, "Blake, I love your spirit. That is why we're here—to find answers, not just to commiserate. What do you suggest we do?"

"I'm not sure. But I am committed to doing something," Blake said. Several others nodded in agreement. "I'm going to engage my staff to work on some potential solutions."

"Haven't you done that already?" Betsy Roberson, head of the global nonprofit, asked.

"Not really," Blake confessed. "I knew it was an emerging issue, but until recently, I was unaware of the magnitude of the situation. Honestly, when Martha announced our topic for tonight, I was hoping one of you had already figured it out."

"Nope!" Bart laughed. "I was hoping the same thing. That's why it was number one on my list."

"No answers," Martha sighed, "but at least we had a good dinner."

"I know we agreed to address a different topic at each meeting, but could we talk about this again next month?" Blake asked.

"Only if you guys bring some solutions," Martha said in a tone that made the group feel they all had homework to do.

◦ ◦ ◦

At home, Blake's son Clint opened the handwritten letter. It arrived looking like the more than 7,000 miles it had traveled, dusty and crumpled on the edges. He knew immediately it was from his friend Baako—the primitive block letters composing the address were the final clue. The two had met on a school trip last spring.

Clint was only sixteen, but thanks to his father's influence and insistence, he already had done more than most his age. One of the adventures Blake had sponsored for his son was to travel to an emerging country. Blake's father had placed a high priority on global awareness and had done the same for him when he was a teenager. A consequence of this exposure was a level of compassion and empathy hard to get any other way.

As Clint read the letter, his eyes filled with tears.

"My little sister Amara died today. I wanted to tell you. She considered you a friend. They say it was the water that killed her. . . ."

Clint thought, *"How can that be? The water? How is that possible?"*

In an instant he remembered, there was *no water* in Amara's village. She walked several hours every day to find water. Clint's pain intensified when he realized she probably had carried the contaminated water that took her life.

He was angry, frustrated, and confused all wrapped up together. He knew he couldn't help Amara, but he also knew he had to do something.

◉ ◉ ◉

Blake was driving home from dinner with the CEOs when he received the call from Clint telling him about his letter from Baako and Amara's death.

"I understand. I know you want to do something. Of course, I'll help. Tomorrow's Saturday. Let's you and I go out for breakfast and talk about options."

Do Something

The next morning, Blake was up before the sun. As he was thinking about how to best help Clint process his emotions, he remembered the pain he felt when his father died unexpectedly. Clint had never experienced the loss of someone he knew personally.

When they arrived at their local pancake house, they were given a corner booth surrounded by seventy-five years of memorabilia and fading photographs of former patrons.

"Do you know my dad and I used to eat here?"

"Yeah, you told me the last time we were here."

"Oh, did I tell you we had our *last* conversation here?"

"No, I didn't know that. What did you talk about?"

"Leadership—and I think we're going to talk about the same thing today."

"We are?"

"Yep. We're going to discuss what you can do in response to Amara's death. I'm guessing the answer will involve leadership."

"Whose leadership?" Clint asked.

"Yours," Blake said. "What have you been thinking?"

"First, I want to get a well for Baako's village."

"Okay, sounds like a good start; then what?"

"I don't know. But I'm going to start with the well. I did a little research, and we can dig one for about $8,000."

"Okay . . . ," Blake waited.

"I ruled out asking you and Mom for the money, and I thought my college fund was out of the question. However, I decided I don't have to do this on my own."

"I'm listening."

"I'm going to ask some of my friends to help."

"What does that look like?"

"Initially, we're going to need to get jobs."

"Who is we?"

"Tyler, Olivia, and Alex. They don't know about Amara's death, but I've asked them to come over this afternoon. They were all there and saw the living conditions and I'm sure they will help. I've done some quick math—depending on where we work, and if we can get a few other contributors, we should be able to raise the money in just a few months."

● ● ●

"What's up?" Alex said with a huge smile. He was the first to arrive at Clint's home. "I don't know if you've ever texted: 'We're having a meeting' before. I don't go to a lot of meetings."

"Well, you'll find out more in a few minutes. We'll start when the others arrive," Clint said in a tone that reflected the weight he felt in his heart.

"Okay . . . others? Who else is coming?"

"I invited Olivia and Tyler, too."

"Cool. This sounds serious, though."

Before Clint could respond, the others walked in.

"Hey, guys," Alex said. "Didn't know you were coming to the *meeting*," he ribbed Clint.

"Well, it did seem odd," Olivia admitted. "It also seemed rather serious. Is everything okay?"

"No. I'm afraid not. Have a seat," Clint said.

"Are you sick? Do you have a disease?" Tyler asked.

"No, I'm fine—well, I'm not fine. Do you guys remember Baako and Amara?"

"Sure. Those two were amazing, and that was the trip of a lifetime," Olivia added.

"Well, ..." Clint paused. "I received a letter yesterday from Baako. Amara is dead."

"No way! She was young—like our age!"

"What happened?" Olivia asked.

"The water," Clint said, without looking up.

"The water?"

"Yeah, do you remember the water?"

"Not really," Tyler admitted.

"That may be because (a) there was *no water* in Amara's village, and (b) we were told not to drink the water they did have."

"Man, that's awful."

The group sat in silence. With tears rolling down her face, Olivia asked, "What are we going to do?"

"That's why I called this meeting," Clint said.

"What can we do?" Alex asked.

"I've been doing some research. The first thing I want us to do is buy a well for Amara's village," Clint said.

"You can do that?" Olivia asked.

"Yes—if you have the cash," Clint responded.

"How much?" Tyler asked.

"About eight grand," Clint said.

"Whoa, that's a lot of cash!" Tyler said in disbelief.

"I know," Clint agreed.

"Any ideas on where we get that kind of dough?" Alex asked.

"Yes. We're all going to get summer jobs," Clint said in a matter-of-fact tone.

"Jobs?" Tyler said. "I've never had a real job."

"You're old enough to start," Olivia said.

"How do you go about getting a real job?" Tyler asked.

"That's the next item on our agenda," Clint said.

Over the next hour, the newly formed team identified more than a dozen places they might work. The list included many of the usual suspects for a summer job and a few outliers—a bakery, coffee shop, several restaurants, an appliance store, a pet grooming salon, two construction companies, a hospital, three clothing stores, a transportation company, and a school.

They divided the list based on interest and potential fit. Each would visit one prospective employer, learn what they could, find out if they were hiring, and report back to the group.

● ● ●

At dinner, Clint updated his family on the plan to buy a well. Blake and his wife Megan pledged their support. Kristen, his sister and eighteen months his junior, said she wanted to help, too.

Clint also told the family about the businesses he and his friends were going to visit in search of their jobs. "We're going to check them out and meet again to compare our notes before we make our final decisions."

Top Talent

Monday morning, Blake called a meeting with the leaders from Human Resources.

"In our last meeting, you brought to my attention your concern and our challenge in finding enough qualified candidates to meet our growth projections. How are we doing on that front?" Blake asked.

Charles, the head of HR, spoke for the group. "Well, since it's only been two days since we met, the situation really hasn't changed much. We have continued to run the play. We're planning to attend a job fair this week, checking our online sources, and we did call a couple of professional recruiters."

"'Running the play' has run its course. It's not working. We need to call a new play," Blake said firmly.

"Do you have a new play in mind?" Charles asked.

"I think we need to go back to the drawing board and ask some different questions. Here are a few to get you started. . . .

"What is our people strategy? Who is our target employee? How would you describe him or her? I've heard you use the term 'Top Talent.' I'm fine with the term—let's just be sure we all agree on what it means.

"Next, what do they want in a job?"

"Who?"

"Top Talent," Blake responded.

"Well, we've never really asked them. We have our offer, our package—you know, fairly standard benefits: medical, dental, vacation, etc."

"We've already established whatever we're currently offering is insufficient or we wouldn't be in this mess. Here's the bottom line: I want to know what it would take for us to become a Talent Magnet."

Puzzled by the phrase, Charles asked, "What's a Talent Magnet?"

"A place so attractive, Top Talent will be standing in line to work here."

What's a Talent Magnet?
A place so attractive, Top Talent will be standing in line to work here.

"Who are you referring to? Leaders, I assume," said Peggy, the junior member of the team.

"No, not exactly," Blake clarified. "I'm thinking more about individual contributors. Granted, many of these talented individuals may someday lead others, but I don't think that should be our focus."

"Don't we know money is the ultimate Talent Magnet?" Gary, another of Charles's team members, asked.

"Sure, people want to make money. But I'm not sure money is the primary motivator for Top Talent," Blake said.

"What do you think it is?" Charles asked Blake.

"That's what I want you to figure out."

"Got it," Charles said. "We'll start by interviewing our own Top Talent. Why are they here? What attracted them?"

"Sounds like a good start," Blake said. "I have one more suggestion."

"And that is?"

"Interview the typical talent, too—men and women we might consider the B players. I think the magic may be found in understanding the differences between the two groups. We want to create an organization that attracts more Top Talent."

"A Talent Magnet," Charles affirmed.

"You got it," Blake said.

❂ ❂ ❂

During the next week, Charles and his team began their search to answer Blake's question: *What does it take to create a Talent Magnet?* The work was divided into two segments: qualitative and quantitative. There would be interviews and an online questionnaire for both typical and Top Talent with the foundational question: *Why did you decide to work here?* The team not only wanted to know the answer to the question, but, as Blake suggested, they wanted to know if the attractors for Top Talent were different from typical talent.

Charles would conduct the initial focus groups personally. The first would be with some of the organization's brightest stars—both newcomers and long-term performers.

● ● ●

After brief introductions, Charles began. "Thanks for coming today on such short notice. As you may have heard, we are trying to attract more people like you to join our organization. So, it seemed appropriate to ask you why you decided to work here. We know men and women of your caliber could have chosen to work anywhere.

"I want to start by asking you to think back to your last job. If you would, please tell us how working here is different from your previous employer. Now, don't be mean. No throwing rocks at your former boss." Everyone laughed.

A middle-aged woman named Carolyn spoke first. "At my former job, I was just a pair of hands. I understood the work needed to get done, but there was no opportunity to grow, improve, or advance. Just hit the numbers, and by the way, the numbers you need to hit are going up—again."

Then, Rob, a younger man, said, "This is my first job, but I came here because of my perception of leadership. I had heard about Blake and the other leaders. Blake actually gave a presentation at my school. After his talk, he hung around and I had a chance to meet him. It seemed like he was a real genuine guy."

"How many of you knew something about the leadership here before you started?" A couple of hands went up. "Okay, thanks. What had you heard?"

"I had never met Blake, didn't even know his name, but my neighbor told me about one of the supervisors here—said he was a stand-up guy, really cared about his people."

"Anyone else care to share why you left your previous company?"

Stan, the oldest guy in the room, said, "It was always about the bottom line. I know companies have to make money. I want them to so we can stay in business. But really? Does it *always* have to be about cutting costs and boosting profits?

I got tired of it and left."

"So, why are you here? We want to make money, too," Charles probed.

"Yes, and I already said, I think that's good. However, this place does good way *beyond* making money. You know, all the things we do in the community. We give back. I think that matters—it's why I'm here."

"Thanks, Stan. Let's hear from the rest of you. . . ."

For the balance of the session, Charles's questions zeroed in on what, specifically, attracted these talented men and women to the organization.

◦ ◦ ◦

The next group assembled was comprised of a diverse group of what the team called typical talent. These were not bad performers; on the contrary, they were good, steady contributors. These were the people some organizations would call their B players. Blake's suggestion to talk to them was about to pay off.

"Hi. For those I have not met, I'm Charles, the head of Human Resources. Thanks for taking a few minutes out of your busy day to have a conversation with me. As you know, and in large part due to your hard work, we are growing. The challenges of growth are numerous. One of them is attracting enough people to get the work done. That's what we want to explore today. What attracted you to work here?"

Charles did a masterful job asking one good question after another. The conversation flowed freely. There were clearly similarities between the two groups, but there were also stark differences. Some of the attractors mentioned by Top Talent were totally absent from the second conversation.

Although there would be more focus groups, based on these two alone, Charles felt Blake's instinct

was correct. The attractors for Top Talent did appear
to be different, but Charles wanted some additional
input before he reached any final conclusions.

⚬ ⚬ ⚬

To collect the hard data, Charles and the team
created a list of potential attractors, many of which
were identified in the early focus groups. They then
built an online questionnaire so that employees
could rank what they felt were the most compelling
factors in their decision to join the company. He sent
the survey to two groups: Top Talent, as identified by
three consecutive years receiving the highest performance ratings; and typical talent, those whose ratings
were consistently just below the Top Talent group.

The survey would be administered to both groups
the following week. The team was anxious to see if
the hard data would support the stories they were
hearing.

To probe deeper, Charles contacted a dozen of
his peers in organizations large and small across
the country. He asked them if they wanted to do the
online survey with their people. The response was
overwhelming—almost all of them said yes.

This broader sample would help establish the
validity of the hypothesis and remove the inherent
bias of any single organization. The team was about
to find out the truth about Top Talent.

Why Top Talent?

Blake was eager to attend the next dinner meeting with the CEOs. Although the previous meeting had been relatively uneventful, he was optimistic. He knew these men and women were in their respective positions for a reason. He wanted to learn as much as he could from them.

After the normal pleasantries, Martha kicked off the conversation with a question.

"Who has a status report for the group? Who's had a breakthrough?" After a long pause, "No one? Certainly, someone has done something." Martha turned to Blake. "You were full of vim and vigor when we first met. What have you accomplished?" she asked.

"Well, we've defined the goal," Blake offered.

"And?" Betsy asked.

"And, we're working on it."

"Doesn't sound like much progress to me," Bart said.

"Well, I understand why you would say that, and I wish we had accomplished more; however, I believe a problem well defined is half solved."

"So, you think you know the problem? I do, too," said Sam Caldwell, the head of a small hotel chain headquartered in their town. "I need bodies; I can't find enough of them."

"That may be your problem, but it's not mine," Blake said. "Our problem is fundamentally different."

"I thought you were struggling to find people," Sam challenged.

"We are, but our problem is *not* finding bodies; we're looking for Top Talent. And the problem we're trying to solve is this: What will it take to attract them?"

"Top Talent sounds like a load of sh-. . ."—Sam caught himself—"crap; it sounds like crap to me," Sam said.

"Hold on!" Martha stepped in. Having known Sam for decades, she felt very comfortable confronting him. "Have you had too much to drink *already*? You're more rude than usual tonight. Listen to the young man."

"Thank you, Martha," Blake said. "I don't know what else to say, really."

"Tell us why you want Top Talent and not just any 'body,' as Sam put it," Martha suggested. "Wouldn't Sam's approach be easier?"

"First, am I alone here? Does anyone else want Top Talent?" Blake asked the group.

Several raised their hand.

"Thanks. That makes me feel a little better," Blake said. "Okay, let's try to explain to Sam why he may want to rethink his strategy and set the talent bar higher. Can we come up with ten reasons Top Talent matters?" Blake spotted a flip chart in the corner of the meeting room. He decided to capture the ideas from the group—he didn't know if he might need them to convince the skeptics in his own organization.

"Okay," Blake said, "ten reasons we would invest the time, energy, and resources required to go after Top Talent. . . ."

A spirited conversation followed and yielded the following list:

Why Top Talent?

1. Creates competitive advantage
2. Is more agile
3. Produces better results
4. Responds well to complexity
5. More growth-oriented
6. Represents our brand well
7. Accelerates growth
8. Creates our future
9. Creates energy
10. Attracts more Top Talent

"Good work. I want to add one more thought. It's why I think the pursuit of Top Talent is our only viable alternative. The growing demands of our customers, increased competition, and the complexities of our business necessitate higher levels of talent. We believe the organizations with the most Top Talent will ultimately win the day."

"That's a convincing argument and an impressive list; so, what are you doing to attract Top Talent?" Betsy asked.

"Honestly, not nearly enough, and to be completely transparent, I'm not even sure what we should be doing."

"Why do you say that?" Martha asked.

"We don't even know what Top Talent wants—not yet. We've begun a project to find out. Unfortunately, we've never asked them. We've just made a lot of assumptions, and based on the current state of affairs, I would say our assumptions have been dead wrong."

Bart said, "Hold on, Blake; you're young, but this is not your first rodeo. You know Top Talent wants top dollar. It's that simple."

"Is it? Is it really?" Blake pushed back. "We lost several candidates recently at the offer stage. We checked. They went to competitors for comparable wages; and one, for less!

"I agree, people want to be paid, Top Talent included, but I'm fairly sure money is not the solution. Unless you just want bodies. I actually think Sam can fix his short-term problem by paying a couple of bucks more per hour. No, I'm not sure exactly what they want, but Top Talent is different. I'm convinced it will take something different to attract them."

Top Talent is different. I'm convinced it will take something different to attract them.

"Please keep us posted," Betsy requested. "Martha, I know you didn't envision this as a single-topic roundtable, but with your permission, can we talk about this again next month?"

"Unless we decide to throw money at the problem or lower our standards, I don't think we have a choice," Martha responded. "We'll see you next month. More answers, *please.*"

After almost everyone was gone, Sam approached Blake and said, "Can we talk?"

"Sure."

"I'm sorry. I know I was out of line, and no, I had not been drinking. What everyone said really makes sense. I didn't want to say anything to the group, but we are *really* struggling. I guess that explains my tone. I know it doesn't excuse my behavior, but I wanted you to know, it was not personal. I've been lashing out at everyone—my employees, my family. I even shouted at a guest last week."

"What's going on?"

"Just what I said. I am so short-staffed, I don't sleep. I'm either working or worried about work. This talent thing is killing me. Literally, I'm afraid."

"What's your plan?" Blake asked.

"I don't have one. I just know something has got to change or I'm done. I thought about what you said—closing the staffing gap by raising my starting wage. I think we would just get more mediocre performance and a weaker bottom line. What I really want is to hear more about what you're learning. Can I call you? Maybe come for a visit? Since I'm in the hotel business, I don't see any conflict of interest, do you?"

"No, I really don't. I'll let you know when we have something to share."

The Search

Monday afternoon, Clint and his friends spread out across town to begin their job search. They had no idea how different their experiences were going to be.

Olivia was thrilled about her first visit: a local clothing store. Fashion was her passion. As she walked in, the woman behind the counter made no eye contact; she couldn't, she was transfixed by what appeared to be a YouTube video on her phone. Olivia wandered through the store for a few minutes and finally approached a clerk and asked if there was a manager on duty. The young girl pointed at the woman watching the video.

"Is it okay to interrupt her?" Olivia asked.

"Are you going to buy something?"

"No, I was going to ask her about a job."

"Why would you do that?" The clerk gasped. "Run, girl, run. You don't want to work here."

"Why not?"

"No respect, no appreciation, a lot of screaming. . . . I've been here for three months and she still calls me 'girl.' I swear she doesn't even know my name."

"Why do you stay?"

"I get 50% off the clothes," she grinned.

"Okay, thanks for the heads-up," Olivia said as she quietly left the shop, convinced the manager never knew she was there.

● ● ●

Alex loved coffee, so when Clint suggested they get jobs, he was convinced the coffee shop was his spot. When he checked in to see if they were hiring, they told him they were always looking for good people. He was encouraged by the barista to go online and complete the application.

"Hey, before you go, let me do two things for you," the young man said.

"What's that?"

"Let me offer you a free drink and introduce you to the manager."

"Okay, thanks."

While Alex was waiting for his drink, a woman approached him and introduced herself. "Hi, I'm Laura. Brad tells me you might be interested in a job here."

"Maybe. I'm doing research at this point."

"If you have questions, here's my card. And, if you have time, I would love to ask you just one question today."

"Sure!" Alex replied.

"Why do you want a job?"

Alex told Laura about Amara's death and the plan to buy a well. She was impressed.

"Thanks for considering us for a summer job. If you decide to come back in, I want to tell you how we are making a difference in the world. It's a story you might enjoy."

"Thanks!"

● ● ●

Tyler had a sweet tooth, so he had chosen the bakery as his first visit. When he asked if they were hiring summer help, the manager replied, "Well, yes, we are. All we can get."

"I'm glad you're hiring. If you don't mind me asking, why are you hiring 'all you can get'? Is business that good?"

"Certainly not. We just can't keep help. So, my approach is to hire everyone who walks in. We'll know in a few days if it's going to work or not. If not, well, I give everyone who leaves a free box of doughnuts—except that kid I caught stealing."

"Why do people leave?"

"I don't know. Maybe because the work is hard, or I'm a real jerk. It could be a combination of the two," he smiled. "If you want to work here, no need for an application. I'll pay you $1.00 above the minimum wage."

"Thanks for the offer. I'll follow up after I consider my options."

"Okay, since you're such a tough negotiator, I'll pay you $2.00 more than the minimum and all the doughnuts you can eat."

Tyler thought there was something a little unnerving about the man's desperation but thought all-you-can-eat doughnuts would be hard to beat. "Thanks! I may be in touch."

○ ○ ○

Clint visited the first of several restaurants on the team's list. It was a large, family-oriented establishment, table service only. Since he was visiting in the afternoon, the place was a ghost town.

The few employees he could see looked busy. After standing at the front for a few minutes, he walked toward the back where someone noticed him.

"Hi, are you here to eat or drink beer?" a young lady asked.

"Well, I came in to talk about a summer job."

"Jim! Kid wants a job!" the employee shouted at the top of her lungs. "He'll be out here in a minute. Want a beer?"

"No, I don't think so."

"Just checking." She smiled and wandered off.

A moment later, a very large man wearing a black tank top and a cowboy hat appeared. He looked at Clint and said nothing.

"Hi, are you Jim?" Clint asked.

"I am, and what's it to you?" The man seemed angry and Clint wasn't sure why.

"Nothing, sir. I just wanted to know if you are the right person to ask about a potential summer job?"

"That would be me," the man said sharply. "Here's the deal: Dishes—60 hours a week. No overtime. Minimum wage. One meal per day, a free beer when you arrive, and another when you leave at the end of the day. When can you start?"

"Well, thanks for the offer. I'm just beginning to consider my options," Clint said respectfully.

"Options!" he exclaimed with a chuckle. "Hell, you got no options here. Take it or leave it."

"I think I've got all the info I need. Thanks for your time."

As Clint turned to leave, Jim said, "Enjoyed meeting you—the offer stands. You can start anytime. Just come on in and grab an apron. No background check."

Huddle Time

The group had agreed to meet on Saturday to process what they had learned and to consider their options.

As Clint's friends arrived, he was discouraged. He knew there were other places to work, but he had been underwhelmed by his first visit.

As soon as the four were seated, Clint said, "I hope you guys had more luck than I did."

Each member of the group shared his or her own experience. The caliber of leadership and the lack of engagement were recurring themes with Alex's experience as a clear outlier.

"It sounds like there are a lot of crappy jobs out there," Clint said.

"I agree, but we don't have to take them," Olivia said.

"We don't?" Tyler said.

"No, we can work where they meet our demands," Olivia said.

"Sounds good. What are our demands?" Alex asked.

"I'm not sure, but we are bright, talented, energetic, and available. We should be able to find someone who will give us what we want," Olivia insisted.

"I'll ask the question again: what do we want?" Alex said.

"We want to buy a well," Tyler said.

"Yes, Tyler, but we want more than that," Clint suggested.

"We do?" Tyler was confused.

"Yes, we do," Olivia added.

"Give me an example," Alex said.

"Okay," Olivia sat silent for a moment with a determined look on her face. "I don't want to work for a crummy boss. I've heard my dad talk about how difficult that is. He says as hard as he works, he realizes the leader is not only the lid on his career—she is the lid on the entire organization. That is so sad to me—for the people, the leader, and the company." She paused again. "I want a **Better Boss**."

"Me, too!" Clint said. "Better than what I've seen thus far."

○ ○ ○

At dinner that evening, Clint shared with his family. "It is really amazing. We've only visited a few of the places on our list, but what has blown me away is how casual some of these people are regarding hiring.

"What I don't think they realize is that we have a part in this decision. When we were talking today about what we wanted in a job, Olivia called them 'our demands.' I wouldn't go that far, but I would call them expectations."

"Very interesting," Blake said as he was immediately transported to his challenge in the war for talent.

"Clint, what are your expectations?"

"We're working to answer that question ourselves. For now, all we know is that we want a **Better Boss** than the ones we've met thus far. When we figure it out, I'll let you know."

Panning for Gold

Charles and Blake were meeting weekly to discuss their talent crisis. Blake knew from experience: focused leadership energy creates impact. Besides, this was his organization's most pressing issue. Where else would he want to invest his time?

"Good morning," Blake said. "Any updates or insights?"

"I've been thinking about how to move this work along as quickly as possible, and because we're both huge fans of benchmarking, I think we should visit a few companies known for having outstanding people. Maybe we can learn from their experience. If we can discover some tactics that have helped them attract Top Talent, it could accelerate our efforts."

"I can support that. You find them, and we'll visit them." Blake said.

● ● ●

After some research, Charles's team found several organizations who had solid reputations for outstanding people. Each company they contacted agreed to allow a visit.

Blake and Charles were set to make their first visit with Clare Fremont, the chief people officer of a midsized company with a predominately hourly workforce.

Focused leadership energy creates impact.

"Clare, thank you for agreeing to meet with us. We've heard so much about your company over the years," Charles said.

"We've heard about you guys, too. We don't usually allow visitors from other companies, but with all you've done to help your people create a high-performance organization, we thought a visit would probably help us more than it would help you."

"Thanks. We've realized, in the complex world in which we live, the game is changing and we're trying to change with it," Blake said.

"I have a lot of questions about your approach, but I will let you go first. Your message indicated you want to talk about talent," Clare said.

"Yes, for all the strides we've made as an organization over the last few years, talent—specifically, finding enough Top Talent—has proven to be a huge challenge."

"Welcome to the club!" she said with a smile.

"We want to know how you attract so many amazing team members. I've met several of them. They are phenomenal."

"You are kind. But, it's not really as you described it."

"Which part?"

"We don't attract a disproportionate share of talented team members."

"You don't? You could have fooled me."

"We may have fooled you. I hope you're not going to stand up and leave when I tell you the truth about our amazing people. Are you ready?"

Hesitating, Charles said, "I guess."

"Let's go back and establish two things. One, we do have phenomenal people. Two, we don't *attract* more A players than anyone else."

"That's where I'm confused. So, how do you do it?"

"I call it 'panning for gold.'"

"Panning for gold?"

"Yep, that's our strategy. The idea was inspired by the way gold was often found in frontier days. The miner would begin by sifting through a lot of rock and rubble; when he found something that looked promising, he would wash off the mud and see if there was gold underneath. If not, he tossed the stone aside and kept searching."

"Okay, tell me how that translates to your people strategy."

"We hire everyone we can get our hands on. We hire with little regard to any predetermined criteria. We hire people every day if we can. Then, we fire quickly."

"How quickly?" Blake asked.

"Sometimes on the first day, often at the end of their first week. I know it sounds harsh, but we can usually tell in a week."

"And, this is your strategy for people?" Charles asked in disbelief.

"Predominately. We do some light leadership development, but we're really panning for gold there as well. We prefer to find leaders who get it without much help from us."

"Wow. That gives us a lot to think about."

The truth: both Blake and Charles knew they had no further questions about Clare's approach. They did not believe a "panning for gold" strategy would give them the sustained results they were pursuing.

More Than a Job

Olivia decided to give retail clothing another chance. Today she would visit a boutique located in a beautiful Victorian-era house just off Main Street. When she arrived, she was greeted promptly by a stylish woman in her mid-thirties.

"Hi, I'm Olivia. Is there someone here I could talk to about a summer job?"

"That would be me. I'm Marissa, the store manager."

"Are you hiring?"

"Maybe," Marissa said with a wry smile.

"That's an interesting response," Olivia said.

"Well, the truth is, yes—yes, we are, for the right person. We don't just hire to be hiring."

"What's the process?"

"It begins with an application; then there are two or three interviews."

"Will I interview with you?"

"Maybe," Marissa laughed. "I don't mean to seem cryptic. However, you will only interview with me if the first two interviews go well."

"Oh, I see."

"Do you have any questions for me at this point?" Marissa asked.

"Just a few. Do you have time now?"

"Yes, let me ask someone to cover for me."

In about ten minutes, Olivia had all the information she needed to take the next step.

"Thanks for your time today! I'll complete the online application and I hope to see you again in interview number 3," Olivia said.

* * *

Tyler was headed to the construction company on his list. He knew the work would be hard, but he loved building things. He met with Daryl Chatsworth, the owner's son.

"Hi, I'm Tyler. Thanks for meeting me without an appointment. I'm looking for a summer job."

"No appointment—no problem, Timmy. We're always looking for people to help out around here. Business is booming!"

"My name is Tyler, sir. Can you tell me about the job?"

"Sorry, sure. You would be a helper."

"What does a helper do?"

"They help," Daryl said with no sign of a smile.

"Is that it?"

"That about sums it up, Toby."

Tyler decided not to correct Daryl this time. "Who would I report to? Who would be my boss?"

"That would be hard to say."

"Why?"

"Your job would be to help the entire crew—electricians, plumbers, carpenters, stone masons, etc. They would all be your boss, or I guess boss*es* would be more accurate."

"Sounds like a big job."

"It is. Any other questions?"

"Just one. Why do you enjoy the building business?"

"It's really simple, Trevor. I don't like people—young, old, rich, poor, don't even care that much for my own family. That's why I like building. I get along good with concrete, wood, and tools—I love tools. Thanks for asking, Thomas. Do you want the job?"

"I'll follow up if I decide to complete an application."

Tyler left the meeting with one overriding impression: "I think 'Doug' makes the guy at the bakery look like a really good boss!"

● ● ●

Alex had been so impressed on his first visit, he went back to the coffee shop. Once again, he had a good conversation with Laura.

"You've been generous with your time—thank you. I have one more question."

"Sure."

"How would working here help me prepare for my future?"

"What do you mean? I thought you were just looking for a summer job."

"I am, but I want to make a good decision. What do you think I would learn during my time here?"

"How would working here help me prepare for my future?"

"Wow! Those are deep questions. Honestly, I could make up some answers, but you've stumped me. I focus on running a good business, but I'm not really focused on *your* future."

"That's okay. No judgment here. I just want to know what I would be getting myself into."

● ● ●

Clint's second visit was to a pet grooming salon. He had always loved animals and thought he might someday make a career as a veterinarian. He called ahead to schedule a visit with Samantha Davis, the owner of the business.

"Good afternoon," Samantha said. "Thanks for coming by. You said you were looking for a summer job?"

"Yes, I'm looking at my options."

"Look no further. This is your summer job."

"What makes you say that?" Clint was surprised by her confidence.

"There is no better place for you this summer. This is the opportunity of a lifetime."

"Why would you say that?"

"I'm going to hand you the keys."

"You are?"

"Yes, sir. You can start the first Monday after school is out."

"What does 'Hand me the keys' mean?"

"It means you will be in charge. Think of all you'll learn."

"In charge of everything?" Clint gulped.

"Yes, indeed: hiring, firing, scheduling, inventory, grooming the animals, customer complaints—not that there would be any. Think of it as a crash MBA."

All Clint could focus on was the word *crash*. "Well, I appreciate your confidence in me. But, I don't know anything about pet grooming."

"They're just dogs and cats. What can go wrong? You'll figure it out. What do you say?"

"I think I'll call you back if I decide to move in this direction." Clint was trying to make his exit as quickly as possible.

● ● ●

The group reconvened at Clint's house.

"Well, any insights?" Olivia asked.

"I'm not sure what you mean by 'insight,' but I had a new thought," Alex said.

"What's that?"

"I think I want more."

"More what?" Tyler asked.

"I don't know, exactly. When I had my second meeting with Laura at the coffee shop, I asked her about my future."

"You did?"

"Yeah, I'm not sure why. It just seemed relevant."

"What were you thinking?" Clint asked.

"Well, what if our summer jobs could help us years down the road?"

"Is that possible?" Many concepts eluded Tyler. "Say a little more."

"It's not fully formed in my mind," Alex said, "but regardless of what I do this summer, I want it to add value long-term. I want it to make sense."

"What does 'make sense' mean?" Tyler asked.

"Okay, here's an example: Olivia has said many times over the years, she sees herself working in the fashion industry. So, it makes perfect sense to me for her to work in a clothing store."

"I get it. That's actually why I visited a pet grooming business—I've considered becoming a vet," Clint said.

"Okay," Tyler was beginning to catch on. "But what if I don't know what I want to do regarding my career? I'm guessing a lot of people have no idea— particularly young people."

"I think what we're talking about is still relevant," Clint said.

"How?" Tyler asked.

"Well, the bigger idea seems to be about a place where we can learn and grow. Maybe you can learn life skills."

"What do you consider life skills?" Olivia asked.

Clint responded, "I don't know . . . maybe some people stuff, how to communicate better, or problem-solving skills. Any of these would probably be helpful regardless of how your career goes."

"So, do we have another 'demand'?" Alex grinned at Olivia.

"Maybe. How would we say this?"

"A place to grow?" Alex said.

"An opportunity to learn?" Oliva suggested.

"I don't really want to learn and grow," Tyler said. "But I do want to be successful in the future."

"How about a **Brighter Future**?" Alex asked.

"I like it!" Olivia said.

"Let's see if we can find a place to work with a **Better Boss** *and* somewhere to help us prepare for a **Brighter Future**," Clint said.

"That would be amazing!" Alex said.

"Anything else, while we're making our list?" Olivia asked.

"Maybe. . . ." Clint hesitated.

"What?" Olivia asked.

"I want more than a job," Clint said. "I think I want to be part of something bigger."

"A bigger company?"

"No, the size of the organization doesn't matter," Clint said.

"'Something bigger' is not going to make the list unless you can tell us more," Olivia said.

"I know. I'll keep thinking about it," Clint said.

Diamonds in the Rough

Although their first visit had not been very helpful, Blake and Charles decided to try again. This time, they would see a small business with a reputation for remarkable people.

"Good morning!" Blake said with a huge smile. "I'm Blake Brown; this is Charles Jones. Thanks for agreeing to meet with us."

"Oh, the pleasure is all mine," the young man said, introducing himself as Mateo. "I Googled you and found out you guys are a big deal, and your company is hugely successful."

"Don't believe everything you read on the Internet," Charles said.

"No, I believe it's *all* true," Mateo said with an impish grin.

"You are correct, about one thing: we are very fortunate to have been on a really good run. Our sales, profits, and customer satisfaction numbers continue to climb—for now," Blake added.

"Why do you say 'for now'?"

"That's the reason for this visit and others like it. We are struggling to attract enough Top Talent to meet our plan. If we can't figure this out, I am not so sure about the future of those health indicators.

"So, as I was saying, that's why we're here. We want to learn from you. How do you attract such amazing talent?"

"I don't."

"Excuse me," Blake said, while thinking, *"Oh, no, here we go again."*

"I don't attract amazing talent."

"The people we've met this morning tell a different story. Based on my initial interactions, they appear to be stars!" Charles said.

"Thanks, but I'll say it one more time: I don't attract amazing people."

"How do you explain your people?" Charles asked.

"I make them great."

"Really? What's your approach?" Blake asked.

"I call it 'diamonds in the rough.'"

"Please, tell us more," Charles said.

"You probably know an uncut diamond has some worth, certainly. However, the real value of the stone skyrockets after it has been cut and polished. I just select people who I can cut and polish until they shine. Like I said, I make them great."

"Yea, but what happens if they turn out to be just a lump of coal?" Blake said.

"You know every diamond starts that way. All it takes is time and pressure. I can provide both," Mateo smiled.

"Do you have other leaders who are master 'diamond cutters'?"

"No, not really. It's extremely hard to do, and since I love it and I'm good at it, it's just become my primary role around here."

"Is what you're describing a coaching role?"

"I guess you could think of it that way, but it's more 'extreme coaching.'"

"Time and pressure?" Charles laughed.

"You called it—I never let up."

☺ ☺ ☺

On the flight home, Blake was eager to compare notes with Charles.

"Okay, two visits, two big surprises," Blake said.

"Totally," Charles agreed. "Sorry to send us on a wild goose chase."

"I think your team asked the wrong question when looking for places for us to visit," Blake suggested.

"You do?"

"Yes, I think they were searching for organizations who *have* outstanding people. That's what they found! However, we're looking for something different—a subtle but real difference. We are trying to learn how to *attract* the best people, not learn how to make them great or just weed out the bad ones. The outcome may be similar, but the process we're trying to create is fundamentally different."

"I agree," Charles said. "It's like a champion sports team: they still develop people, but the best teams always try to recruit the best athletes."

We are trying to learn how to *attract* the best people, not learn how to make them great or just weed out the bad ones.

"Exactly!" Blake said. "I still believe in developing people, too. I just want to begin the process with the *absolute best talent possible.* Mateo's diamonds in the rough strategy can work, I guess, if your organization is really small or if you have a lot of leaders like Mateo.

"Regarding panning for gold, that would be far too costly for my tastes."

"I agree—it would certainly be costly financially, but I think the larger cost might be in morale. It feels like the culture could easily become transactional or, even worse, toxic." Charles said.

"So, what have we learned?"

"We know a few things we don't want to try—and I'm more committed than ever to building a real Talent Magnet!"

Breakthrough

The kids were gathered for their next meeting. With summer quickly approaching, Clint was becoming more impatient every day. He had hoped each of them would have jobs by now.

"Okay, how's it going?" Clint asked.

"I think I'm there," Olivia said. "I'm ready to apply."

"How about you, Alex?"

"Same here. I love coffee. And, I think if I push a little and apply myself, I can learn some things to help me with my future. They just haven't focused on that much in the past."

Clint turned to his longtime friend. "Tyler?"

"Well, I hope you guys won't be mad."

"What did you do?" Olivia asked in her best schoolmarm tone.

"I got a job."

"Congratulations!" Clint said.

"Well, we'll see," Tyler said.

"Where are you going to work?" Alex asked.

"The bakery."

"Really? The guy told you he was a jerk."

"I know. But I love doughnuts, it's just a summer job, and he's willing to pay $2.00 above minimum wage," Tyler said as his voice crackled with excitement.

"I can see how he got you," laughed Clint. "Okay, that's good—one down and three to go."

"I'm going to apply on Monday," Olivia said.

"Me, too," Alex said. "Clint, what are you going to do?"

"I've got to keep looking. My pet grooming experience was scary. By the way, *never* take your dog to that place!"

◉ ◉ ◉

Clint decided to call ahead rather than just show up for his next visit. When he did, he was told there would be a group interview on Monday afternoon. He felt like he really just wanted to talk to someone but thought, *"What the heck?"*

On Monday, he was greeted by an energetic young man in his mid-twenties. "Good afternoon!"

"Hi, I'm Clint. I'm here for the group interview."

"Glad to have you! If you'll take a seat, we'll start momentarily."

Clint waited with about ten other people until the owner came out and introduced himself. "Hi, I'm Julie. I'm glad you are here. We have a process in place to help us both determine if this is the best place for you to thrive. We only want a win-win relationship. I know most of you will not make a career here. That's fine with me. Our goal is to help you learn skills that will serve you the rest of your life."

Clint reviewed his mental checklist. *Um, I may have just had my questions answered about the boss and the future in 15 seconds. I wonder what's next?*

Our goal is to help you learn skills that will serve you the rest of your life.

Julie continued, "I'll not be leading you through the process. I have talented leaders to do that. However, if all looks good, we'll meet again in your final interview."

The candidates were first divided into small groups. After introductions, each potential employee was asked to share his or her ideal job, followed by a couple of questions about prior work experiences. Then, the final question: "Why is this job important to you?"

At the end of the hour, one of the facilitators stood and said, "Thank you for coming today. We appreciate you investing the time to help us learn more about you. Here's our promise to you: each one of you will receive a call within twenty-four hours regarding next steps. We wish the best for each and every one of you. Thanks for coming."

As Clint was leaving, Julie caught up with him in the parking lot. "Clint, have you got a minute?"

"Yes, ma'am."

"I know you were told you would hear back from us soon regarding your next steps. Have you got time for another interview today?"

"Yes, I do. Who will I meet with?"

"Me."

"Really?"

"Yes, I am the final interview for all our employees."

"That sounds challenging. Don't you have hundreds of employees?"

"I do. However, I really can't think of anything better to do with my time. Certainly, my team helps a lot. But I know if we get the people part right, everything else is much easier. If you have time, let's go find a place to talk."

If we get the people part right, everything else is much easier.

Clint was intrigued as Julie shared her vision for the business, the people, and the community. She talked about core values and what motivated her. She talked for almost an hour.

Julie concluded by asking, "Do you have any questions for me?"

"Several, here's the first: why did you decide to tell *me* all of this?"

"What do you mean?"

"I'm sure you don't share that story with everyone. Why me?"

"Oh, you're mistaken. I *do* tell everyone that story. I think it matters. If you are going to work here, much of what I shared needs to become your story, too. If you decide to work here, we have to be on the same side of the rope pulling toward the same goals."

"Okay. That's a lot to process. But it all sounds amazing. Do we have time for a few more questions?" Clint asked.

"Certainly."

Clint proceeded to ask his questions. He wanted to know about his schedule, the amount of flexibility he would have regarding time off, the work he would be doing, how he might learn and grow while working with Julie and the team, and, finally, the starting pay. After listening to Julie's response, he said, "Thanks! What do I do next?"

"If you want the job, orientation begins in ten days."

"I've got the job?"

"If you want it."

"I can start sooner. School is out on Wednesday."

"No. Thanks for the offer; however, no one works without attending orientation. I only told you the highlights of the story. You need a deeper understanding before you serve our guests."

"Okay. I'll take the job." Clint said.

"Oh, one more thing," Julie said as he stood to leave.

"Yes?"

"Sylvia, the leader who facilitated your group, told me about your well project. I want to help."

"You do?"

"I do. We are always looking for ways to give back. I'll commit $500."

"Seriously?"

"Absolutely. Over the last decade, we've been involved in dozens of projects like yours. It would be an honor to partner with you."

"You've got to be kidding!"

"Nope. We'll have a check for you at orientation."

Risky Business

Olivia's first day at work was uneventful. She was surprised by the pace, or lack thereof. The only exciting part of the day was a request from Marissa asking her to work late and do a "little project."

"All you need to do is check in the inventory and put it away. The truck should be here around 6:00."

"Where do I put it?"

"In the store room in the attic. There's not much of a system. Just try to put like items together. It shouldn't take long."

Olivia thought, *"Oh, well, the overtime would be good to have. And, if I do a great job, maybe it will help make a better first impression."*

Although the store didn't close until 6:00, Marissa left at 5:45. Olivia felt a little weird being left alone, but as she locked the front door, the driver rang the back doorbell.

When she opened the door, she could see he already had unloaded four pallets of boxes.

"Hi, I'm Ralph. Are you new here?"

"Yes, I'm Olivia. This is my first day."

"Sorry."

"Sorry for what?"

"Sorry you've got to do this on your first day."

"It's okay. Maybe I'll get some brownie points."

"Sign here," Ralph said, handing her a clipboard.

"Well, should I check it first?"

"What do you mean check it?"

"I was told to 'check in' the inventory. I assume that means check to see we received everything we ordered."

"Do you know what you ordered?"

"No, now that I think about it, I don't."

"So, what do you want to do?"

"I guess I'll sign it."

"Good."

She took the manifest and signed her name, hoping she was not going to be fired after her first day. "Now, how do we get these boxes to the attic?"

"We?" Ralph said. "I'm off to my next stop. That's something you'll have to figure out. That's why I said, 'Sorry.'"

"Okay." Olivia was feeling sick. She knew this 'little project' could take hours. As Ralph drove away, she texted her mom.

> Great news! I get to work late on my first day ...
> Overtime pay sounds good to me ☺

She stuck her phone back in her pocket and began to take the first of many boxes up the three flights of stairs to the attic. She was not prepared for what she saw next.

The attic door creaked as it swung open to reveal a dark, dank space. Because of the pitch of the roof, the attic was a story and a half high; and, for Marissa to say there was no system was an understatement. The place was a mess!

Surveying the situation, Olivia decided she needed to organize a few things and determine, generally speaking, where the various items should be placed. In the corner, she found the tallest ladder she had ever seen—it looked as old as the house and was so heavy. Olivia didn't even know ladders had ever been built out of wood!

She dragged the ladder into place and began her ascent; she was about eight feet off the floor when she heard the crack. The last thing she remembered was the floor approaching fast. In less than a heartbeat, Olivia was unconscious on the floor.

Lesson Learned

The next thing Olivia knew, she was waking up in the hospital. Her mom and dad were both there.

"You took a nasty fall," her dad said.

"Am I okay?"

"Yes," her mom said tentatively.

"What's wrong?" Olivia demanded. She had not yet realized she was wearing a cast on her right arm.

"You are fine. And we are thankful all you have is a broken arm and . . . ."

Olivia looked down and in horror exclaimed, "I have a broken arm!"

"Yes, we know. When you fell, you must have tried to catch yourself. You were just too high off the ground."

"How did you know?"

"We didn't. At 9:00, when you weren't home, we tried to call your cell—no answer. We didn't know your new boss's name or how to contact her, so Dad drove to the store. He found the back door open with inventory on the curb," her mom explained.

"I have to tell you," her dad said, choking back the tears, "I've never been as scared in my life as when I was running up those back steps calling your name. Then, when I found you lying there, ..." He began to cry. "I thought you were dead."

"Dad called 911 and here you are."

"What's next?"

"They want to keep you for a day or two for observation."

"Did you call my boss?" Olivia asked.

"No, I'm going to see her later today and share a few thoughts with her before I offer your resignation," her dad said.

"I guess that was the shortest summer job ever."

● ● ●

The next time the kids gathered at Clint's house, he was thrilled they all finally had summer jobs—except Olivia, who had "resigned." Everyone greeted her with a hug.

"We're so glad you're okay," Alex said. The others nodded in agreement. Then, no one appeared to know what to say next.

"Okay," Clint broke the silence, "what's up with your jobs?"

"I quit," Tyler said.

"What?" Alex said. "You just started!"

"I know. My dad always says if something seems too good to be true, it probably is. The promise of free doughnuts plus $2.00 above minimum wage—I should have smelled a rat."

"What happened?" Olivia asked.

"Well, you remember the owner told me he was a jerk."

"Yeah, I wasn't going to bring that up again," Clint said with a smile.

"Okay, I know, I know. As it turns out, he is more of a jerk when he's been drinking. He was literally throwing things in the kitchen. It was crazy!"

"Okay. Olivia's dad forced her into involuntary retirement, and you quit. Alex?"

"I'm okay. Only had a couple of shifts under my belt, but I think we're good."

"Tyler, I may have an idea for you," Clint offered. "I don't want to speak too soon, but I may have found the perfect job."

"Tell us more about this 'perfect job,'" Olivia said, skeptically.

Clint told them about his group interview and meeting with Julie.

"It sounds super!" Tyler said. "Why wouldn't I apply tomorrow?"

"It goes back to something you said earlier about sounding too good to be true. I don't want you to follow me if this turns out to be a sham. However, I think it's legit."

"What makes you say that?" Alex asked.

"When Julie heard about our well project, she promised us $500!

"Get out of town!" Alex said. "There's no way this woman, Julie, who you just met, is going to stroke you a check for $500."

"She said I could pick it up at orientation," Clint said.

"We'll see," Tyler smirked.

"One more thing," Clint said. "My conversation with Julie made me realize what I've been trying to say the last few meetings. Julie is creating something I want to be part of—even if just for the summer."

"And that is . . . ?" Alex asked.

"A **Bigger Vision**."

"That's it! That should definitely be on our list going forward," Olivia insisted.

"Hold on—just slow down." Tyler was struggling again. "I *think* I understand what a **Better Boss** would look like, although I've only had one boss—for about two hours. And, I can *imagine* a lot of good things when we talk about a **Brighter Future**; but honestly, I have no idea what you're talking about when you say **Bigger Vision**."

"I get it," Olivia said. "Let me try." She turned to look directly at Tyler. "Okay, I'll make this as simple as possible. I agree with Clint: I don't want *just* a job, and I don't think any of us do."

"We don't?" Tyler asked.

"No! We want to make a difference," Olivia said.

Alex jumped in, "And, I don't know about you guys, but I want the *company* I work for to make a difference, too."

"Now that you mention it, that is one of the things that attracted me to the coffee shop. I didn't know how to describe it, but I thought it was cool they were working to make the world a better place," Alex said.

"That sounds really good to me, too," Tyler said. "I just never thought about it like that."

Alex looked at Clint. "So, back to this 'perfect job.'"

"Julie certainly wants to make money, but she also has a **Bigger Vision**; that's why she wants to help with the well," Clint said.

"What's next?" Olivia asked.

"Tyler, if this turns out to be for real, I'll put in a good word for you. Let me check it out first."

"You can put in a good word for me, too," Olivia added. "I don't think my dad is going to keep me on lock-down forever. He said he thought I was dead when he found me." She paused, "So I'm not going to ask for permission to work *anywhere* for a few weeks."

"Anything else, before we go back into the real world?" Clint asked with a smile.

"I've been thinking about our demands, and we missed something on the list," Olivia said.

"We did?" Alex asked.

"I think we need to add the basics."

"What does that mean?" Tyler asked.

"The basic stuff every job should offer," Olivia said, "like a safe place to work."

No one was going to argue with her.

"Anything else we consider a basic?"

"A fair wage, basic training," Alex said. "And to be treated like a human being."

"And not have things thrown at you by a drunk," Tyler added.

"You wouldn't think you'd have to think about these when looking for a job, but it looks like you do," Olivia said.

The Answer

"Good morning!" Charles said at his team's next meeting. "Blake, it's great to have you join us today. We're excited to share with you the work we've done over the last month to answer the question: is Top Talent attracted by different factors than typical talent? The short answer is yes. Before I reveal the differences, let me quickly recap our methodology."

"Quickly," Blake said, forcing a faint smile.

"Yes. We did qualitative and quantitative work on this—focus groups with our own people plus an online survey with people around the country. Was that quick enough?"

"You're getting better," Blake said with a genuine smile.

"So, the answer is yes—Top Talent is attracted by different factors than typical talent."

Charles went to the board and wrote:

Attractors . . .

Top Talent	Typical Talent
The Basics	The Basics

"First, in both camps, we have the basics," Charles said.

"Okay, hold on—you said the attractors were different," Blake pushed.

"There are some differences; there also are some things both groups hold in common. You can think of these as table stakes. You must provide these things to even be considered by either group."

"Are we going to talk about what 'the basics' means?" Blake asked.

"We can come back to it, but the short answer is fair wages, adequate training, roles that interests them, tools and resources needed to perform their job, etc."

"Okay, I'll let you finish filling in the chart, and then we'll talk."

Charles continued, calling out each attribute as he wrote.

Attractors . . .

<u>Top Talent</u>	<u>Typical Talent</u>
The Basics	The Basics
Culture	Culture
Brand/Reputation	Brand/Reputation
Leadership	
Personal Growth	
Values & Mission	
Impact on Society	

When Charles finished, he stepped back and looked at the board.

"Help me interpret this," Blake said.

"The implications for us are mixed but promising."

"Tell me more," Blake said.

"Let's start with the items in both columns. What this means is that *all* potential employees value these things: the basics I mentioned earlier, plus an organization's culture, and their reputation in the world—their brand. I think we're on solid ground on these three."

"I would think so," Blake agreed, "but I want you to say a little more about culture. It feels like it would be the most important thing on the list."

"Culture is very important—that's why it is on *both* lists. However, it's not the most important factor to *attract* Top Talent. If your culture is not positive, healthy, welcoming, and vibrant, you'll have trouble finding anyone to work for you. Everyone we've talked to agrees with you, Blake—culture is critical.

"But, let's look closely at the items that appear only in the Top Talent column. *These* are the attributes most valued by the best performers."

"Hold on. Are you telling me typical performers don't value leadership and growth?" Blake asked.

"Not exactly," Charles began. "In the columns, we have the items that *attract* each group. Leadership and personal growth do not *attract* typical talent. They may be appreciated and even valued to some degree, but they don't usually draw typical talent to an organization.

"Here is the bottom line: when we provide the things *most valued* by Top Talent, we dramatically increase the likelihood they will want to work for our organization.

"And," Charles concluded, "I mentioned our standing was mixed on these items."

"Yes, I was waiting on you to circle back to that," Blake said.

"Well, you know we've had trouble landing some top candidates recently."

"Yes, I know."

When we provide the things *most valued* by Top Talent, we dramatically increase the likelihood they will want to work for our organization.

"The problem is right here on this chart."

"Let me guess: we're not doing as well on the items valued by Top Talent?"

"Correct. It's not as if we aren't doing anything; we are just wildly inconsistent across departments and teams."

"What are our next steps?"

"Well, there's one more thing for us to consider. Losing candidates is one problem to solve; getting more folks in the pipeline is another challenge."

"And?" Blake said.

"We believe the primary blockage in our talent pipeline is hiding in plain sight," Charles said.

"And that would be?" Blake asked.

"We've got to do a better job telling the story."

"Exactly which story are you referring to?" Blake asked.

"The story about our leadership, growth opportunities, vision, and impact in the world. We have to be more strategic and intentional about letting the world know what we have to offer," Charles said. "Looking back, we've never focused on this before; we didn't have to—we've always had plenty of talent."

"A story untold, moves no man to action," Blake said.

"Correct!" Charles said.

"I'm assuming we're also going to shore up the cracks so we can tell the story with confidence and credibility," Blake suggested.

"Correct."

"What's the plan beyond that?" Blake asked.

"We're on it. We should have something to share with you next week."

"Looking forward to it!"

● ● ●

The first topic at dinner was Clint's orientation.

"Son, please tell us about your first day at work," Blake said.

Clint shared the entire agenda. He told his family about the vision and mission of the organization. He shared about the growth opportunities he would be afforded in the months to come. He talked about the scholarship program and the free leadership development resources he would have access to. He talked about his co-workers—eight of whom had gone through the orientation with him. He went on and on about the values of the organization and how important it was to serve, on both sides of the counter. And finally, he shared the impact his new organization was having in the community and around the world.

"Oh, I almost forgot, Julie also gave me the $500 she promised during orientation!"

Blake was dumbfounded. He said, "Clint, you and your friends have been trying to decide what you wanted in a job."

"Yes, sir."

"What did you decide?" Blake grabbed a napkin and pulled out his pen.

As Clint spoke, Blake wrote:

What attracts top talent?

Better Boss

Brighter Future

Bigger Vision

"Son, this is genius."

"No, Dad, it's just what my friends and I want in a job."

"No, it's more than that." Blake told Clint and the rest of the family about the work Charles's team had been doing. "We have been searching for a way to win the war for talent. We've been trying to figure out what will attract Top Talent—talent like you, and your friends.

"We've been studying this issue for months. You want to know what we've learned?"

He went back to the napkin and added a second column:

What attracts top talent?

Better Boss   ➡️   Leadership

Brighter Future ➡️   Personal Growth

Bigger Vision   ➡️   Mission, Values, and Impact on Society

"Honey, I hate to tell you," Megan said, "but I like the way the kids said it a lot better."

"Me, too!"

"Dad, one more thing," Clint said. "We did talk about adding something to our list."

"Let me guess," Blake said.

"Okay, what do you think?" Clint said.

"I'm guessing it has something to do with the basics."

"No way! How did you know?" Clint asked.

"We have a lot of smart people working on this, and we've been listening to Top Talent. They agree with you: the basics are critically important. However, we don't believe they give us a competitive advantage."

"Just a real disadvantage if you *don't* provide them," Clint added.

"Yes," Blake said. "What's on your list of basics?"

"After Olivia's accident, a safe place to work."

"That makes sense. What else?"

"We haven't given it a lot of thought, but we did talk about competitive pay."

"That makes sense, too. If we want Top Talent, we probably shouldn't start our pitch by saying, 'Work here and we'll pay you *less* than what the market is offering.'"

"Yeah, that would be crazy," Clint laughed. "You may also want to include something about basic training, but beyond those few things, it feels to me like a focus on the big three would go a long way to attract good people," Clint said.

"I think that's an understatement. If you can deliver a **Better Boss**, a **Brighter Future**, and a **Bigger Vision**, you can become a real Talent Magnet.

"Thanks, Son, for helping give language to something that is going to serve our organization for years to come."

Next Steps

Blake was eager to share Clint's insights with Charles; he didn't want to wait until their next scheduled meeting. So, he sent a text:

> Please stop by my office TODAY.

"Good morning," Charles said. "What's up?"

Blake shared with Charles his entire conversation with Clint. He even had the napkin as a visual aid.

"What do you think?" Blake asked.

"Fascinating and validating," Charles said.

"I get the fascinating part, although I might have chosen a different adjective. What's the validating part?" Blake asked.

"We have been trying to determine what attracts Top Talent. Clint and his friends are exactly who we want to attract, just a few years from now. They are bright, articulate, energetic self-starters. Olivia and Clint are dueling for valedictorian, aren't they?

"Yes, they are," Blake said.

"They are Top Talent! That's why I say 'validating,'" Charles said.

"Okay, let's say you're right: their work validates our own. What's next?"

"Let's assume we adopt their language: we work to provide a **Better Boss**, a **Brighter Future**, and a **Bigger Vision**. That would become the heart of employee value proposition or our 'promise,'" Charles suggested. "There are certainly other elements of the promise; some of those we've discussed recently— fair wages, competitive benefits, a vibrant culture, etc. But the *featured* message probably needs to be the attributes that will attract the best people."

"What would we do with the 'promise'?"

"Two things: one, we work to be sure it is true consistently throughout the organization. We know we have work to do on this part. Next, we would work diligently and strategically to tell the story."

"I guess we'll add the Promise to orientation?" Blake asked.

"No, probably not," Charles replied.

"Why not?"

"If we believe we know what will *attract* Top Talent, we want to tell the story *before* they are hired. In orientation, you are preaching to the choir— they're already on board!

"I think there's one more thing we have to do," Blake said.

"What's that?" Charles asked.

"If we are going to make the promise of a **Better Boss**, a **Brighter Future**, and a **Bigger Vision**, we need to be sure our leaders know their role. They are the ones who will ultimately deliver on the promise or not. Without their daily commitment, all we'll have is an empty promise. Can you and your team help identify some of the key leadership behaviors we'll need to embrace to make it all real?"

"Absolutely! I'm headed to a team meeting right now—we'll get started."

❍ ❍ ❍

Charles joined his team meeting in progress. Peggy, Kim, Ben, Gary, and Rose were all present.

"Thanks for starting without me. I've been with Blake," Charles said.

Kim said, "We're at a good point for you to give us an update."

Charles told the team about the validation they had received on their work from Clint and his friends and the way they described what they are looking for in a job.

Ben, the senior member of the team, spoke first. "I really like their angle; the language the kids came up with is much more approachable than the path we were on—but I've also got a question. Are we surprised that these high school kids reached the same conclusions we did? I mean, really—we're professionals with years of training, education, and experience. It just seems, well, . . . bizarre."

"It makes perfect sense to me," Peggy said.

"Why is that?" Charles asked.

"The attractors of Top Talent are not age-bound," she said.

The attractors of Top Talent are not age-bound.

"Do we have any data to support that?" Rose asked.

"I think we do," Peggy said. "If you look at our data, both qualitative and quantitative, what Top Talent wants doesn't really change over the course of their working life. The only difference we see is a slightly lower importance given to personal growth opportunities later in someone's career. Other than that, it appears the attractors of Top Talent are universal."

"Even for high school kids, it appears," Rose added.

"What do we do now?" Kim asked.

"Regardless of what language we use, our first priority must be to deliver the promise," Rose added.

Ben said, "I agree: if we sell it, we've got to deliver it."

"I think this Talent Magnet idea will certainly help us attract more talented people, but it will probably have another effect," Charles speculated.

"What's that?" Peggy asked.

"If we consistently deliver the promise, I bet people will stay longer," Charles said.

"I think we've already seen this in a few departments," Rose said.

"And, don't forget, for this 'magnet' to have any effect, people must know what we're doing here," Ben said.

"I agree with you all," Charles said. "But there's one more piece of the puzzle. We not only have to create the culture we're describing—we have to sustain it."

We not only have to create the culture we're describing— we have to sustain it.

"How do we do that?" Rose asked.

"Blake and I have been talking," Charles began. "We want to expand our assignment. We must be sure our leaders know their role in delivering the promise. Without daily leadership action, all we'll have at the end of the day is an empty promise. So, he's asked us to identify some leadership behaviors or best practices to help us deliver the promise more consistently."

Charles went to the whiteboard and wrote:

Our Assignment . . .

- More consistently deliver the "promise"
- Help the organization better tell the story
- Identify key leadership best practices

Let's begin with a **Better Boss.**"

A Better Boss

"First, we should probably try to look at all of this from the perspective of Top Talent. The real question is not how *we* define these terms, but how do *they* think about each of these phrases?" Gary suggested.

"That is the right question," Rose said.

"So, let's calibrate," Kim suggested. "Exactly who are we targeting with this message?"

"Top Talent, A players—call them what you will, but they represent the group of consistent top performers. To be included in our quantitative study, these women and men had received the highest performance rating for the last three years," Charles said.

"Yes, I remember," Gary said. "It was a little depressing."

"Why was that?" Rose asked.

"I didn't qualify," he said with a straight face.

"That's okay," Charles said. "Ninety percent of our people didn't. We set the bar really high."

"It sounds like we're in agreement; we are targeting consistently high achievers."

"I don't like it any more when you say it that way," Gary said.

"Get over it," Rose quipped.

"So, what do these high achievers want?"

"A **Better Boss**."

"Better than what?"

"Better than a typical boss, I guess."

"We're going to have to say more than that," Peggy said.

"Let's go back and look at the transcripts from the focus groups. We had scores of comments on leadership," Ben said. "Take a couple of minutes and review the responses."

After a few minutes, Ben asked, "What did people say?"

Peggy jumped in. "I'll go first. I think the comments were overwhelming on this one: a **Better Boss** is caring."

"What comments led you to that conclusion?" Ben asked.

Peggy read aloud some examples:

"My boss asked me about my long-term goals. I've never been asked that before."

"My leader knows my name—and the names of my kids! Do you realize how hard that must be? She obviously cares."

"Before I ever started working here, the leader who interviewed me said he was going to give me a

chance because he thought this place would help me grow. Can you imagine? He didn't say, 'I'm going to give you a job to extract value from you'—he was talking about adding value. That told me a lot about his heart for people."

"My supervisor covered a shift for me recently—he did it himself. He knew my baby was sick. He told me to make my child my first priority. That's crazy. I love that guy."

"I had a hard conversation with a leader recently. She told me I could do better, could achieve more. She offered to help, but she said I had to decide. She cared enough to confront me. And, she's right. I can do more."

"You guys have convinced me. A **Better Boss** is definitely caring," Ben said. "So, what's the leadership behavior we're looking for?"

"How about **Demonstrate Care**?" Rose suggested.

"Sounds good to me," Peggy said. Others on the team nodded. "Let's capture these as we go. Who knows, once we have each concept defined, the leadership best practices may be obvious."

"What else?" Kim asked.

"I had *present*—the data indicates people prefer a boss to be around," Rose said. "Listen to this . . . ."

"I see my leader; this is good for me and the team. He actually shows up and does real work."

"I agree with the idea," Gary said. "I just think the language is too narrow. I like the word *engaged*. The comments to support this were numerous . . ."

"My leader knows what is going on."

"Our supervisors are there for us—on the good days and the bad."

"It's hard to pull one over on our leaders. They are grounded in the realities of the business."

"My leader is willing to help us. He is not above doing the work."

"It's as if our leaders see their role differently than most leaders. In my previous job, it was clear, we were there for our leaders. Here, it's as if they are here for us!"

"If I had a dollar for every time one of our leaders has asked me how he or she could serve me, I would have enough to retire! They genuinely want to create a win-win for me and the company."

"I like it," Peggy said.

"Me, too. *Engaged* is probably a better term," Rose added.

"Let's capture that idea. A **Better Boss** is engaged."

"This may be too simple for the best practice, but what about **Stay Engaged**?" Ben offered.

"I like the simplicity of it," Charles said. "There should be no confusion; absentee leadership is not our approach."

It's hard to pull one over on our leaders. They are grounded in the realities of the business.

"I have one more candidate for the list," Rose said.

"What's that?"

"*Competent*," Rose said. "A **Better Boss** must be *competent*."

"Doesn't that go without saying?" Ben asked.

"I'm not sure," Peggy said. "There are a lot of lousy, incompetent leaders in the world."

"Yes, but hopefully not here," Charles laughed.

"Yes, it's easy for you to laugh," Gary said. "Have you ever worked for an incompetent leader?"

"No, I can't say that I have," Charles admitted.

"Well, I have and it was a nightmare!" Gary said, shivering.

"I suggest we add it," Kim said. "I think Gary is right."

"Hold on." Peggy wasn't satisfied. "If we add it, we need to set the bar higher."

"What do you mean?" Ben asked.

"Competent is not excellent; competent is not exceptional. We're talking about a *better* boss, not an average boss."

"What do you recommend?" Kim asked.

"I like 'skilled.' I want a leader who actually knows *how* to lead," Peggy suggested.

"I like it," Rose said. "So, we want our leaders to be skilled. How would we describe the leader's responsibility here?"

"How about **Lead Well**?" Gary suggested.

With obvious agreement, Kim said, "I'll add it to the list."

A Better Boss

- Demonstrate Care
- Stay Engaged
- Lead Well

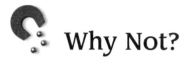

Why Not?

On Monday morning, Blake received a text from Sam. Although he had promised to follow up after their last meeting, Sam thought a nudge was appropriate.

> Love to meet—you name the time and place.

Blake was going to be near one of Sam's hotels later in the week, so they agreed, a short meeting was possible.

● ● ●

When Blake and Sam arrived, the lobby restaurant was empty. After being "greeted" by an indifferent hostess, they were told to pick any seat they wanted. "It's not like we're expecting a crowd," the young lady said. Both men grimaced. Then, rather than escort them to a table, she just pointed to the wide-open dining room.

After finding a table in the corner, Blake was waiting to see what Sam would say about their hostess.

"It's awful, I know," Sam said apologetically. "That's what we get—attitude and a high level of indifference. I told you, this is killing me," he sat leaning on the table with his face in his hands.

After a moment, Blake asked, "Has it always been this way?"

"I don't think so—not really." Sam's response was unconvincing. "I mean, none of my properties has ever been a five-star establishment, but I don't remember it being this bad."

"Why not?"

"Why not what?"

"Why haven't your properties been awarded five stars?" Blake asked.

"You don't understand our industry."

"You are correct, I don't. But tell me why your hotels aren't recognized in your industry?"

"There are a lot of reasons."

"Name a few."

"We don't have golf courses and spas, for starters."

"Okay, let's use the term *five-star* figuratively, not literally. If you rule out the facilities, what's the difference?"

"I know where you're going," Sam admitted. "It's the people. I don't have five-star people."

"Why not?"

"Again, a lot of reasons."

"I'd love to hear a few of those reasons," Blake said.

"First, it's impossible to get high-caliber people to do this type of work."

"Really?"

"Yes, virtually impossible."

"Well, it seems like some of your competitors have figured it out."

Sam paused, realizing Blake had a point. "Okay, maybe they have, but I could never afford the caliber of people we're talking about."

"Are you sure?"

"Of course. My margins are razor-thin. Any increase in wages really hurts."

"Okay, but what if better people—we call them Top Talent—could help you raise the top line? Let's face it. We've not even ordered yet, and based on the way we were treated when we arrived, I'll probably not come back. How is that good for business? And, based on our research, you don't have to outspend your competition—you've just got to be competitive. It's not really the money that attracts the brightest and the best." Blake proceeded to explain the findings from their work.

"Okay, even if what you say is true," Sam said, "I don't have time to focus on Top Talent. I have a business to run."

"You do. And I think you told me and the others at the meeting, finding people is your top priority. How much time are you personally investing in your top priority?" Blake let the question sit for a moment before he continued. "And, how many full-time people do you have dedicated to work on this issue?"

"Well, my managers are always scouting for talent."

"You mean the women and men who actually run the hotels?"

"Yes."

"How much time do you think they devote to the issue of talent on a daily or weekly basis?"

How much time are you personally investing in your top priority?

Sam was stuck. Blake's questions had boxed him into a corner. He had never connected all the dots before. He didn't believe he could attract or afford the people he said he wanted. and his beliefs were driving his behaviors—one of those unconscious behaviors was not allocating people to help solve the problem.

"I don't know what to say," Sam admitted. "That's why I wanted to talk."

"Listen, I'm not judging you. You heard me confess at our last meeting: we're not yet doing all we can to solve this problem either. However, it starts with a decision. Leaders set the talent bar for their organization.

"If you want Top Talent, you have to decide. Intention is key to unlocking a whole new world of possibilities. It was intention that enabled us to put men on the moon, create self-driving cars, and discover cures for countless diseases. And, intention is the first step for any leader who wants to win the war for talent. We only solve the problems we intend to solve."

A Brighter Future

At the team's next meeting, they reflected on their work to clarify the idea of a **Better Boss** and felt good about their efforts. They believed making the necessary behaviors specific would help the leaders throughout the organization engage and deliver the promise.

"Next on our agenda, 'A **Brighter Future**,'" Kim said.

Gary was the first to comment. "You don't have to be Top Talent to know what that means."

Rose asked, "What do you think it means?"

"More cash, of course," Gary snorted.

"Gary, are you still singing that song? You obviously haven't looked closely at the data," Ben said.

"Money is not the panacea you want it to be," Peggy said.

"And, it was rarely mentioned as an attractor during the focus groups," Charles reminded the group.

"Why do you think that is?" Rose asked. "We all need money."

"Certainly, Top Talent expects to be paid. However, this **Brighter Future** they seek is really about more than money," Charles said.

"Okay, if it's not about the cash, I don't know where to go from here," Gary said.

"What do they want?" Ben asked.

"I think they want us, or whoever they work for, to help them *prepare* for a **Brighter Future**. What we're really saying is that we will help you get there—we're making a promise to help them live into *their* preferred future."

"I think you're right. Our question then becomes how can we help? What are the enablers of a **Brighter Future**?" Ben said.

What are the enablers of a *Brighter Future?*

Referencing both the data and the comments from the focus groups, the team created a very long list of contributing factors, or enablers, for a **Brighter Future**.

After staring at the board for a minute, Rose said, "I see a pattern—wait, that's not it. I see several patterns."

"I think I see it, too," Ben said.

"There are probably three categories represented," Rose began.

"Right, and the first has something to do with growth," Ben added.

"I see that," Peggy said. "You can combine personal and professional growth with stretch assignments and new skills."

"Okay," Kim said. "Let's call it *growth*."

"Don't forget, we need to identify leadership behaviors and best practices. What do the best leaders do pertaining to growth?"

"We expect it, demand it, encourage it, foster it, nurture it—help me here," Kim said, running out of ideas.

"That's an impressive list, but it feels too soft," Ben said.

"Soft?" Kim raised her eyebrows.

"Yeah, if we're telling Top Talent they can count on a **Brighter Future**, how do we communicate a little more intensity?"

"How about *champion*?" Rose said.

"I like the word *champion*," Kim said.

"That's more like it," Ben said.

"Let's call that our first leadership behavior: **Champion Growth**."

"Before we move on, are we sure we know what we mean, or what Top Talent means, when they say they want to grow?" Kim asked.

"I think they want transferable skills," Rose said.

"What does that mean?" Gary asked.

Everyone just looked around the table, and then Charles said, "Peggy, what do you think it might mean?"

"Well, I think it means people want to learn things that have application beyond their current role."

"I think you are correct, and it may even mean they want to learn things to serve them beyond their time with our company," Charles added.

"So, let me get this straight," Gary began. "'Top Talent,'" making air quotes with his fingers, "wants us to train them for their next employer?"

"Well, I don't know that I would have said it exactly like that, but yes, our brightest and best understand they may not be in a single role for the rest of their career; they also realize they may not even stay with us forever. Therefore, before they ever sign up in the first place, they are thinking about their future, and one of the things they want to know is how working here will make them more employable down the road," Charles said.

"I thought that," Peggy said, immediately checking the reaction of the team. Then under her breath she said, "Did I say that out loud?"

An awkward silence enveloped the room. Peggy was new and very talented. Charles, trying to defuse the situation, jumped in. "Outstanding!" he said. "Help us here. What was going through your mind as you considered a job here as it relates to your future?"

"Honestly, it was exactly as you described. I don't know how many jobs I'll have in my career; I don't even know how many career changes I'll make over the next 40 years! What I do know is the statistics show *very* few people stay at one company for a lifetime. Therefore, it seems prudent to think of each job as a learning opportunity. If a person is thoughtful and diligent, he or she can amass quite an education simply by choosing the right places to work. If you end up somewhere that doesn't encourage and facilitate growth, you could lose a few years of development. That's a real opportunity cost."

"Thanks, Peggy. I suspect several of us have had similar feelings during our career journey thus far." Turning her attention back to the group, Kim continued, "So, does **Champion Growth** cover these transferable skills Top Talent wants?" She saw a nod or two and said, "Okay, we'll move on."

"What else can leaders do to help someone realize a **Brighter Future**?" Ben continued.

"Looking back at the list of candidate behaviors and activities, I like the words *challenge* and *opportunity*. Can we find a way to combine them?"

"I think *challenge* and *opportunity* are different. I like them both, but I wouldn't try to force them together," Charles added.

Rose said, "So, if we treat them separately, what would the leadership behavior be for challenge?

"The best leaders **Provide Challenge**," Kim said. The group agreed.

"Now, how about opportunity?"

"They also **Promote Opportunity**," Ben added.

What's the difference between these last two? Rose asked. "They seem very similar to me."

"I'll try," Peggy said. "I think **Provide Challenge** is more about today—stretch assignments, coaching, candor, and hard conversations, if needed. And, calling out the best in people."

"That makes sense to me," Charles said.

"**Promote Opportunity** feels more future-oriented," Peggy continued. "Being sure people know about other roles and assignments within the organization would be an example. Holding talent loosely. We've challenged our leaders across the business that talent belongs to the organization, not the department. This could help."

Talent belongs to the organization, not the department.

"Okay, I think that works. Thanks for those examples," Rose said.

"Are we together on this?" Kim asked while scanning the room. She decided yes, except Gary; he looked more disengaged than usual. "Gary, are you okay? Do you agree with our list of behaviors?"

"Listen, I'm still struggling with this whole idea that we need to cater to hotshot talent like Peggy, who is not going to be committed to the long-term success of this company," Gary said.

Charles was about to speak when Ben beat him to it. "Two things: first, you need to apologize to Peggy, right now."

"I'm sorry, Peggy. My comments were not about you, just the whole idea. It seems wrong to me."

"Second," Ben continued, "I think you've really missed the point on this one. Nothing has been said, or is intended, to imply that people who see their job as a platform for growth are any less committed to the company than you are. In fact, the growth mindset men and women like Peggy bring to this place is refreshing and challenges me personally to give my best every day."

"Well, . . . ," Gary stammered.

"One more thing, you aren't the only one who doesn't currently meet the definition of Top Talent. They didn't ask my opinion, either. However, I am going to work as hard as I can to help this place be successful as long as I take a paycheck."

Kim took a deep breath and said, "Candor is good. Thanks to all of you for sharing your perspective. I think we need a break—let's take 15 minutes," she said.

As everyone stood to leave, Kim walked to the board and wrote:

A Brighter Future

- Champion Growth
- Provide Challenge
- Promote Opportunity

Validation

Clint was now through his orientation and ready to work. Driving to his first shift, his mind was racing.

Could this place be all he thought it was? The orientation had made him even more convinced it was a unique company. The owner herself had led about two hours of the four-hour session. Clint could still feel Julie's energy as she shared her vision and invited each new team member to be part of something much bigger, a story of impact far beyond the walls of the business.

Clint arrived about fifteen minutes early; he didn't want to be late. When the shift leader realized Clint had already arrived, he greeted him by name although the two had never met.

"Good morning, Clint. Glad to have you on the team. My name is Matt. I'm one of the team leaders here. I'll help you get started today."

"Thanks, Matt. I have a question. How did you know who I was?"

"Other than your name badge?" Matt smiled.

"Oh, yeah, I'm not used to wearing one of those."

"Here's how." Matt pulled out his phone and showed Clint a photo of himself.

"Where did you get that?" Clint asked.

"From orientation—they took your picture, remember? It was sent to the entire leadership team. We don't want you feeling like a stranger around here."

"Pretty cool," Clint said.

"Speaking of not being a stranger, why don't you clock in and let me introduce you to the team who's already here today."

Matt introduced him to about thirty-five people. The most amazing part of the experience was he shared something personal about every one of them.

"How come you know so much about everyone's personal lives?" Clint asked.

"That's part of my job."

"Seriously?" Clint said. "You must have a broad job description."

"Not really. My primary role is to serve these people—help them, and the business, be successful. It's extremely difficult to serve people well if you don't know them."

"What's next for me?"

"I want you to meet some of our customers."

"Okay. How do we do that?"

"We go out front and talk to them."

"Do you know them?"

"Many of them. We have a lot of regular customers."

The two young men walked through a door into the retail portion of the business. The first woman they saw greeted Matt by name. "Matt, how are you today?"

My primary role is to serve these people—help them, and the business, be successful.

"I'm pumped."

"About what?"

"I have a new team member here. His name is Clint."

"Hello, Clint. It's good to meet you."

"Mrs. Smith," Matt said, "you'll find this interesting. I know you've been to Africa several times."

"You have a good memory, Matt. Yes, I've been to Africa many times."

"Clint is buying a well for a village there."

"I like that! Please tell me the name of the village."

After a ten-minute conversation with Mrs. Smith, she gave Clint her email and said she wanted to help. All Clint could think was *"This place is crazy!"*

Matt introduced Clint to about a dozen other customers. By the end of the customer tour, Matt said it was time for Clint's first break of the day.

"Break from what?" Clint said as he laughed. "I haven't done any work yet."

Matt corrected him. "No, you're mistaken. You started working with the first person you met this morning. I know this sounds crazy, but we're really in the people business."

After a short break, Matt reappeared with a young lady. She looked to be a few years older than Clint and had a big smile.

"Clint, this is Madison, your trainer. She will help you create a training plan and begin the process of teaching you how to do what we do. Any questions?"

"Just one for now."

"Shoot!" Matt said.

"How long will the training take?" Clint was thinking in terms of minutes. He was eager to get to work. Matt's response shocked him.

"Initial training, based on your schedule, about three weeks."

"Matt, you do know this is only a summer job?"

"We do. But who knows? Maybe you'll stick around," he smiled.

Clint looked at Madison, who said, "Most folks do."

"Okay, I'm ready," Clint said.

As they were about to walk away, Matt said, "Oh, two more things. Madison, be sure to have Clint back at the office at 4:00. He has a meeting with Julie. And, Clint, here's my cell number if you need anything." Matt handed Clint his card.

"*Am I dreaming?*" Clint thought.

Clint could already tell Madison was sharp. He said, "What's your story?"

She explained to Clint she had started working here when she was only fourteen years old.

"Can you do that, legally?"

"I had very limited hours and tasks—but it was a start."

"How did you know about this place?"

"My family came here often when I was little. That's when she hooked me. Julie used to tell me and my parents she wanted me to work here someday. She told us if I would start my working career here, she would help me make my dreams come true. When I was fourteen, I told my dad I wanted a job. He said, 'Okay, call Julie for an interview.' The rest is history," she smiled.

"What's your dream?"

"Still figuring that out, but Julie and all the leaders here are committed to my success. I can't think of anywhere else I would want to work at this point in my life."

❀ ❀ ❀

At 3:50, Madison said, "We need to head back to the office. Matt said you were going to meet with Julie."

"What's on the agenda?"

"Not totally sure, but I'll give you a heads-up."

"What's that?"

"She may ask you if you want to stay."

"Are you kidding me?"

"No, I'm serious. This is more than a job for her, and she wants to know that you really want to work here. Hey, it's not for everybody. The work is hard and the hours are long."

"I'm staying."

"Glad to hear it. Here's my card."

"With your cell number?"

"Sure. Call if you need anything. I'll see you at 8:00 tomorrow. And, if you're open to it, I'd like to have lunch tomorrow . . . off the clock."

"Okay."

"I heard something about a project you're doing in Africa or Asia or somewhere. I'd like to hear more about that."

"It's a date. No, I didn't mean it like that. It's not a date—it's a meeting."

Madison flashed a smile. "See you then. Here's Julie's office."

As Clint opened the door, Julie stood and greeted him.

"Good afternoon. How was your day?"

"Honestly, I don't feel like I earned my wages today."

"Why not?"

"I met some amazing people on both sides of the counter, and I learned some things about how to do my job, but I didn't do any real work."

"Here's a good lesson for you to take from your first day: don't ever undervalue preparation. It sounds to me like you had a very productive day."

"I'm glad you think so," Clint said. "And, I wanted to thank you for the time you invested with us in orientation. It was awesome! I feel like you gave us all a real head start."

"My goal is to give you a ten- to fifteen-year head start."

"What do you mean by that?"

"I want to teach you, and all our team members, how to be successful in life and business. You'll learn things here many people at other companies won't be exposed to until mid-career—if at all."

"Why do you want to help us?"

"Someone gave me a head start when I was about your age. I've been trying to pay it forward for thirty years. And, make no mistake: helping people grow and teaching them how to add value to others is extremely good for business.

Make no mistake: helping people grow and teaching them how to add value to others is extremely good for business.

"Are you willing to work hard this summer and learn all you can?"

Before Clint could answer, Julie interrupted. "I'm going to expect a lot out of you. Are you sure you want to stay?"

"Yes, I'm thankful to be here."

"I'm thankful to have you," Julie said as she extended her hand to Clint.

"See you tomorrow!"

● ● ●

When Clint sat down for dinner, he started talking even before Blake and the others could sit down.

"Dad, it was crazy! Matt is my supervisor. He knows everyone by name, and he knows about their life outside of work, too. Then, I spent over an hour talking to customers—about nothing! They tell me we're in the people business. Then I met Madison— she's my trainer. They said I would be in training for *three* weeks. I reminded them this is a summer job. They said I might stay longer. I had a meeting with the owner one-on-one at the end of my shift. She asked me if I wanted to stay. She said she was going to expect a lot from me. She said she was thankful to have me on the team! It was off the hook!" Clint said all of this barely taking a breath along the way.

"That sounds amazing! Congratulations, son. It sounds like you've found a real Talent Magnet."

"Oh, yeah," Clint said, remembering their previous conversation. "How's that going?"

"We're making progress, but it sounds like we are waaaay behind Julie and your new team," Blake said.

"What makes you say that?"

"You said you and your friends were looking for a **Better Boss**, a **Brighter Future**, and a **Bigger Vision**. It sounds like Julie has created what you envisioned."

"I think she has."

A Bigger Vision

Blake was anxious to attend the next meeting with his new CEO friends. He wanted to hear the progress they had made on the talent front.

They met in the same hotel banquet room. Déjà vu: each leader once again lamenting the state of talent and sharing the same difficulties he or she had shared in their first meeting. Honestly, Blake was shocked at the lack of progress. Then, it was his turn.

"We've been busy. We really are convinced our organization can become a Talent Magnet—a place so compelling, Top Talent will line up to work for us."

Earl Bannon interrupted and said, "Sounds like the youngster has been smoking something they don't sell at the corner store." A few laughed at Earl's attempt at humor.

"Not tonight, sir. But I can tell you what we've been doing. We're trying to determine what it takes to build a Talent Magnet."

"Did you figure it out? Don't keep us in suspense— I'm not a young woman," said Mrs. Livingston.

"Well, I think we have."

"Do any of you know what Top Talent really wants?" Blake asked.

"Cash?" someone asked.

"They do want to be paid a fair wage, but that is *not* what really excites them, and it is not what will keep them. Top Talent wants three things: A **Better Boss**, a **Brighter Future**, and a **Bigger Vision**. That's what we're working to give them. The extent to which we are successful in this endeavor will determine our organization's success over time."

Blake's brief comments sparked a candid and often heated conversation. There were many questions. Blake answered the ones he could; others, he admitted he didn't know the answers—yet.

"Still sounds crazy to me," Ed said.

"I'll tell you what's crazy—*hoping* things will get better." Blake's energy ticked up a notch. "Hope is not a strategy.

I'll tell you what's crazy— *hoping* things will get better.

"My son is sixteen years old. If he were graduating from college today, I'm fearful—no, I'm confident he would not want to work for my company. That is unacceptable to me.

"My organization needs more Top Talent. I'm thankful their demands are simple: to be led well, to live with the hope and promise of a better future, and to be part of a bigger vision. We can do this!

"And when we do, we'll attract Top Talent from our city, our state, and beyond; we'll create such a compelling force, we'll find men and women from around the world will want to work with us. That's what we're building."

◉ ◉ ◉

At Charles's next team meeting, the first item on the agenda was to continue clarifying the components of a Talent Magnet and the leadership behaviors that would make it all real.

"What's next? I guess we should tackle the **Bigger Vision** today," Ben suggested.

"Sounds good to me," Kim said.

"How should we approach this?" Rose asked.

"Any ideas?" Kim turned the question back to the group.

"Let's go back to the data on this one. There are focus group comments, but the data is clear and, frankly, surprising to me," Charles said.

"Why would you say that?" Gary asked.

"Here's the truth: if you had asked me before we did this research what Top Talent values, I would have guessed that both leadership—**Better Boss** and personal growth, **Brighter Future**—would be at the top of their list. But I would not have predicted that a **Bigger Vision** would be that important."

"Why is it important?" Ben asked.

Kim pulled out the data file and projected it for everyone to see.

As they sat looking at the screen, Ben said, "Who can interpret this for us?'"

Rose said, "I can. As it relates to this facet of a Talent Magnet, there were two things that stood out when comparing top and typical talent.

"First, when asked to rank the factors that would *attract* them to work for an organization, the mission and values of the organization mattered *significantly* more to Top Talent than they did to typical talent.

"The second thing we see regarding the **Bigger Vision** is that Top Talent wants the opportunity to make a difference. We have interpreted that to mean a difference in the world."

"Yes, the actual question on the survey pertained to 'making a difference in society,'" Gary added.

"Top talent has more of a future orientation than their counterparts," Kim said. "It comes through over and over again."

"So, when we combine these findings—the importance of mission, values, and the desire to make a difference—a **Bigger Vision** appears to be a good way to represent these ideas," Rose concluded. "I think Clint and his friends got it right again!"

"Does this make sense to everyone?" Ben asked.

"I think so. Let me try to play it back a little differently," Kim said. "Top Talent wants a real connection with their employer—more than just a paycheck. They want to be part of something *with* their employer. That's why the mission and values matter to them.

"Right," Rose said, adding, "They want a personal resonance with the organization—not just a transactional relationship."

"Also, if you're a person who wants to make a difference in the world, wouldn't you want to be part of an organization that feels the same way? It feels like an alignment issue to me," Gary said.

"So how do we communicate what we just talked about in a few words?"

"I'm struggling a little with how to proceed," Kim said.

"What if we start with the leader's role in creating, sustaining, and achieving a **Bigger Vision**?" Gary asked.

"Okay, who has something to kick us off here?" Kim asked.

"Assuming you already have a vision, which we do," Peggy began, "I think one of the things leaders do is **Ensure Alignment**."

"I think that's clear, but say a little more," Ben probed.

"Well, it seems to me the real power in a vision is harnessing the collective energy of an organization. If everyone is not in sync, you lose a lot of energy, productivity and impact. I think creating alignment is one of the most important things leaders do."

"Any questions remaining on this one? Can we agree, one of the key leadership behaviors to make the **Bigger Vision** a reality is **Ensure Alignment**?" Charles asked.

Creating alignment is one of the most important things leaders do.

Everyone nodded.

"What else?" Rose asked.

"How important is vision to people, really?" Gary asked.

"Well, according to the data, it matters a lot to Top Talent," Ben said.

"Really? I'm still not sure. I know, I know, we have the data; but seriously, I've worked in places where I never even heard the vision. Honestly, I've worked in a few companies that I'm fairly sure didn't even have one," Gary said.

"I think you're on to something," Charles said.

"I am?" Gary said.

"Yeah," Rose nodded. "A vision is of no value if people don't know it. I think that's a candidate for our next leadership behavior."

"Maybe, but there's something more important than knowing," Ben added. "People must feel connected to it—personally."

"What about **Foster Connection** as our second leadership best practice?" Peggy asked.

"I like it," Rose said. "Thank you, Gary, for helping us see that. I would have missed it."

"What's next?" Charles asked.

"I think there's a big idea we haven't discussed yet," Peggy offered. "I think a **Bigger Vision** must be far-reaching."

"Isn't that why we call it a *Bigger* **Vision**?" Gary asked sarcastically.

"Sure, I get that," Peggy replied. "But here's what the data indicates: top performers want to make a difference in the world. My thinking is fairly pragmatic; if the story is not far-reaching, how big can it be?"

Top performers want to make a difference in the world.

"Does far-reaching need to be thought of as global?" Rose asked.

"I don't think so. Far-reaching can be helping local kids stay in school," Charles added.

"Or helping someone acquire job skills or buy their first home?" Ben questioned.

"Correct," Charles affirmed.

"Now, all this is not to say the impact couldn't be global," Rose said.

"You know what I'm hearing? It doesn't sound like a conversation about reach," Charles said.

"Really?" Kim questioned.

"No, to me it sounds like a discussion about *impact*," Charles said.

"That's it! It's not about *where* you make a difference . . . ," Gary said.

"It's that you make one," Kim said, finishing Gary's sentence.

"That's a **Bigger Vision**. It's about making a difference in this business and beyond," Rose said.

"We've always wanted to add value to people's lives beyond the transaction," Kim said.

"So, help me here: what do leaders throughout the organization have to do with this, anyway? We don't set the vision," Gary said.

"No, but our role is critical in bringing the **Bigger Vision** to life—making it real," Peggy said.

"How?" Rose asked.

"We are uniquely positioned to share our successes. Leaders throughout the organization can make our **Bigger Vision** tangible as we go about our daily work. We can **Celebrate Impact**," Peggy concluded.

"I think that's worthy of the list," Kim said, and the others agreed.

Rose added the final phrase:

A Bigger Vision

- Ensure Alignment
- Foster Connection
- Celebrate Impact

Do It Now

At their weekly update, Blake could hardly wait to tell Charles about Clint's first day on the job.

"Good morning, Blake," Charles said as he walked in the office. "How was last week?"

"Outstanding. I attended a seminar—wish you could have been there."

"A seminar? I didn't hear about it. Were you out of town?"

"No, it was at my house. I learned about creating a Talent Magnet from my son."

"Have Clint and his friends been strategizing again?"

"No, he actually found a job. It sounds like all we've been trying to create."

"Where is it?"

"The other side of town."

"Is it a big place?"

"A few hundred employees."

"What else do you know?" Charles asked.

"I know we have to move faster on this," Blake said. "When my son and his friends graduate from college, they are not going to work for us. They are going to work for people like Julie, Clint's new boss."

"We're on it, Blake. I'm here today to share our latest thinking. We've been working to understand what it takes to create a powerful Talent Magnet." Charles laid it out in a simple equation:

$$TM = B^3A$$

"The strength of our **T**alent **M**agnet is equal to our ability to deliver on our promise: **B**etter Boss, **B**righter Future, and a **B**igger Vision multiplied by the **A**wareness of our promise," he said.

"Where did you get the formula?" Blake asked.

"We were inspired by the real formula for the force, or strength, of a magnet. The B stands for the density of the magnetic field, and A equals the surface area of the magnet.

"In our case, the density of the magnetic field is determined by how well we deliver on our promise—all three elements. Then, rather than *A* for area, we've switched it up to refer to **Awareness**. The parallel is striking: a magnet with a small surface area is weak, and in our case, if awareness is low, we will have a weak Talent Magnet."

"That's interesting—and, it makes a lot of sense to me. What do we do next?" Blake asked.

"We've created a draft of leadership best practices you and I discussed in our last meeting. We know this list is just a start—there are many other ways to strengthen our Talent Magnet. However, we believe having a list of actual behaviors will be huge for improving our execution against the promise. Without our leaders' ongoing and daily involvement, we'll never become a Talent Magnet."

Charles shared the list with Blake:

Talent Magnet
Leadership
Best Practices

Better Boss
- Demonstrate Care
- Stay Engaged
- Lead Well

Brighter Future
- Champion Growth
- Provide Challenge
- Promote Opportunity

Bigger Vision
- Ensure Alignment
- Foster Connection
- Celebrate Impact

After a moment, Blake said, "I have two thoughts. First, I love the list! It moves this idea of a Talent Magnet from a clever metaphor to an actionable plan for competitive advantage. Please tell your team I said thanks. I'll stop by myself soon, but for now, please relay my heartfelt appreciation.

"Second, I agree with something you said a moment ago."

"You do? What was that?" Charles asked.

"You said we would never be able to create a Talent Magnet without our leaders. You are correct. That's why I think these leadership best practices can be a game changer for us. The clarity is refreshing." Blake reached out to shake Charles's hand and said, "Thank you!"

Tell the Story

Charles met with the team to check on their progress and to share his latest conversation with Blake. After the team's typical time of join-up, the first agenda item was Talent Magnet.

"Blake was very impressed with your work on this project—he said thank you! Our ability to attract and keep Top Talent will create a significant competitive advantage for us," Charles said.

"Blake and I have continued to think about how to accelerate our efforts. Here's what I would like us to do: let's divide the work. Ben, Rose, and Kim, please continue to partner with the departments to build action plans for shoring up our execution against the promise. The new leadership behaviors should help. Gary, Peggy, and I will begin working on how we can better tell the story. At the end of the day, the strength of our Talent Magnet really does hinge on **Awareness**.

"We'll meet again next week for updates. Thanks!"

* * *

The group charged with telling the story decided to move to another conference room and continue their meeting.

"Where do we start?" Gary asked.

"So, let me be clear on our assignment," Peggy said. "Ben, Rose, and Kim will work on improving our execution across the organization; all we have to do is tell the world what we have to offer—correct?"

"Exactly," Charles said.

"I think we can finish the plan for that before lunch," Gary said sarcastically.

"No, I think this may be a little harder than we think," Charles said.

"I agree. We aren't going to finish the plan by lunch, but why do you think it's going to be so hard?" Peggy directed her question to Charles.

Before Charles could respond, Gary spoke up. "I'll give you three reasons: the world is a big place; how we talk about the culture is tricky; and frankly, the resources to pull this off may be a challenge as well."

"Okay," Peggy acknowledged the spirit of his comments with a nod and said, "I would like to take those three concerns one at a time, and I think we need to talk about the 'tricky' part first. Why do you say it's tricky?"

"Well, you saw my reaction earlier, which, of course, was way out of line, but it was my reaction. If we tell people we are doing all this work to attract

Top Talent, we could make everyone else feel like second-class citizens," Gary answered.

Charles nodded in agreement. "Well said, Gary."

"Here's how we deal with that. Who is going to fault us, or any organization, for talking about how much our leaders care, the way we help people grow and pursue a bright future, and the good we do in the world?" Peggy said.

"Again, the answer is tricky. It depends on *how* you talk about those things," Gary insisted.

"I know, but assuming we are thoughtful and communicate with a humble spirit, I don't think we'll alienate our staff. I believe this message would make them proud to work here."

"Why is that?" Gary asked.

"Even if people are not *attracted* by the things we're discussing, they are likely not opposed to them. If you are shopping for a car and find one you like, but it has some standard equipment you wouldn't necessarily purchase à la carte, you probably still buy the car. The things we're talking about here will be our 'standard equipment'—they are built in at no extra charge. They may not attract you, but they probably won't repel you, either."

"Should we tell the world we are trying to attract Top Talent?" Gary asked.

"No, we just tell the story: here's who we are; this is what we do; this is what we believe. The magnetic field we'll create will have its greatest 'pull' on Top Talent. If our conclusions are correct," Peggy added, "many looking for work will be indifferent to our message, but Top Talent will resonate deeply with our story.

Many looking for work will be indifferent to our message, but Top Talent will resonate deeply with our story.

"That's our assignment. I propose we acknowledge the 'tricky' nature of this and move forward," Peggy suggested.

Charles and Gary nodded in agreement.

She continued, "Your comment about 'the world is a big place'—I have an idea about that I'll share in a moment."

"What about the resource issue?" Gary didn't want to miss that one.

"At my previous job, my leader used to say, 'Money follows big ideas.' Let's create a jaw-dropping plan and see what happens regarding resources. Besides, I think we can do a lot with what we've already got."

"We don't have much," Gary grumbled.

"We may have more than you think," Peggy said. "My husband is in the military, and I've heard him talk about the concept of force multiplication. The idea, as I understand it, is simple. You find ways to leverage what you already have to greater advantage. Let's see how we can use this idea to help tell our story."

"What do we have to leverage?" Gary said.

"Two things come to mind immediately," Peggy said. "Social media and hundreds of employees."

"Okay," Gary said as more of a question. "I'm with you, sorta. . . ."

"To your point about the world being a big place, the planet is not as big as it used to be thanks to the Internet and social media. Their combined power is mind-boggling. We can use it as a force multiplier if we are thoughtful and deliberate," Peggy said. "We can share our story with millions and millions of people around the world."

"Help me with this. Practically, what could this look like?" Gary asked.

"Okay, I'm just brainstorming, but let's consider our website."

"What about it?" Charles asked.

"Pull it up on your laptop," Peggy said.

Gary and Charles huddled around Gary's screen.

"Tell me what you see," she said.

"What do you mean?" Gary said.

"What does it look like?"

"It looks like a corporate website. What's your point?"

"That *is* my point," Peggy said. "Do you see anything on the first page that would indicate we are a Talent Magnet?"

"Oh," Charles said. "No."

"Anything that would make you think we are serious about our promise: **Better Boss, Brighter Future, Bigger Vision**?"

"No," Gary said.

"Okay, go to our corporate Facebook account and repeat the drill. How about Twitter, Instagram, Snapchat, and whatever next week's hot channel will be? We are not currently using the power of social media to tell our story, but we can!" Peggy exclaimed. "Social media is the most powerful leadership tool in the history of the world. But you have to use it strategically to realize its value."

Social media is the most powerful leadership tool in the history of the world.

"Okay, we've got more here to work with than I thought," Charles said with a huge smile. "Thank you, Peggy, for helping us catch up with technology."

"Oh, don't worry, we'll never catch up—we've just got to be sure we never stop running," Peggy said.

"Okay, you mentioned our existing employees. What have they got to do with this?" Gary asked.

"What if we deputize all of them as our ambassadors?" Peggy suggested. "We could create our own internal speakers' bureau. We could train and equip all our people to tell our story."

"I think the Public Relations team has a slide deck already," Charles commented.

"No!" Peggy said forcefully, with some obvious frustration in her voice.

Both Gary and Charles were caught off-guard by her response.

"What did I say?" Charles asked innocently.

"Honestly, Charles," Peggy said, shaking her head. "I can't believe you would think that."

"Think what? I missed something, too," Gary said as Charles processed Peggy's rebuke.

"You guys are highlighting one of the big challenges we'll have to solve going forward. PR does *not* have a slide deck on our new promise—how could they? What they *do have* is a deck, and probably a video or two, telling our *historical story.* Save it for orientation! It is not going to attract Top Talent."

"Okay, I think I've got it now. Our historical story matters, but the fact we were founded 100 years ago by first-generation immigrants is *not* the story we need to tell to become a Talent Magnet," Charles said.

"Correct," Peggy said. "The main idea here: when we talk about 'telling the story' as it relates to Top Talent, we've got to tell the story *they* want to hear."

When we talk about "telling the story" as it relates to Top Talent, we've got to tell the story *they* want to hear.

"**Better Boss**, **Brighter Future**, and **Bigger Vision**?" Gary said with a slight question in his voice.

"Exactly!" Peggy affirmed.

"This is going to be fun," Gary said.

"Let's create a plan!" Charles added

 # Launch

Now that the pieces were coming together, the team wanted to meet with Blake and share their work. The meeting was scheduled for Monday morning. Blake decided to include the entire executive team as well. He felt he knew enough about the work to broaden the circle and reduce the cycle time for adoption.

"Good morning, all!" Blake said exuberantly. "I'm excited about today."

"Blake, you're excited about every day," Charles jabbed with a smile.

"Now that you mention it, you're right, but even more so today! Let me tell you why. . . ."

Blake set the context for this briefing and concluded his remarks by saying, "Working with people is the most challenging and rewarding part of being a leader. We can never shirk the responsibility. It comes with the job. If we abdicate our people responsibilities, we forfeit our leadership. People must always be our top priority. More than vision, strategy, creativity, marketing, finance, or even technology, it is ultimately people who determine our success. That's why I'm so fired up about this work. We are going to do a better job of attracting and keeping the best people.

More than vision, strategy, creativity, marketing, finance, or even technology, it is ultimately people who determine our success.

"Charles, what do you have for us?"

"Well said, Blake. We do need more Top Talent. And, as we've discussed before, the war for talent is real. However, today, we are not here to talk about the problem; today is about the solution.

"We have done extensive research with Top Talent to determine what they want in a job, and the good news: their demands are simple to articulate, a little more challenging to deliver, but it is possible." Charles asked Kim, Gary, and Peggy to explain each of the core elements—**Better Boss**, **Brighter Future**, and **Bigger Vision**—and the leadership behaviors that accompanied each one.

When the three had finished, Charles continued. "Now that we know what Top Talent really wants, we were able to do an assessment of our current practices. The results were a mixed bag; some parts of the organization are far ahead of the majority, and others are lagging way behind. We are not consistently delivering on what we've shared today. We've already begun working on plans to strengthen each of these areas across the business."

At this point, Christine, the chief marketing officer, spoke up. "What about the parts of the business that are providing a **Better Boss**, **Brighter Future**, and **Bigger Vision**? Are they attracting more Top Talent than other departments who are further behind?"

"Not in every case," Charles said.

"That's where this whole idea breaks down for me. If we know what Top Talent wants, *and* some are *already* providing it, why do they still have a shortage of talent?"

"Fantastic question. Let me respond with a question for you: have you, at any point in your career, witnessed an amazing product, priced fairly, not sell well?"

"Sure. It happens a lot."

"Why?"

Before Christine answered, her expression changed. "I see where this is going," she said with a smile.

"Help us here. Many in the room don't have your background and experience. Why is it that sometimes good products don't sell?"

"Awareness or, more accurately, I should say lack of awareness. People don't buy products they don't know about," Becky said.

"Our conclusion exactly!" Charles then shared the equation the team had created:

$$TM = B^3A$$

"We are recommending we move into the **Awareness** phase of this work. We are going to partner with Marketing, Public Relations, Community Affairs, Training, Leadership Development, and Human Resources to be sure we create and execute a coordinated communications plan to let people know about our promise.

"When we do, . . . ," Charles paused. "Let me close with a quote from one of our focus groups:

"I was like the kid who bought Cracker Jacks for the popcorn. I was delighted when I found the free prize inside! I came to work here because I needed a job, but what I found was so much more. This place has changed my life."

"We want to be sure everyone knows there is a free prize inside—and it might just change your life."

Celebrate!

The summer seemed to pass at a blistering pace; already the days were getting shorter and the kids were talking about going back to school. As Clint prepared to work a Saturday shift, he talked to his mom and dad before he left the house.

"You guys are going to come today, aren't you?"

"Wouldn't miss it," Blake said. "I'm looking forward to meeting Julie."

"Exactly what is going on today that would warrant an invitation from Julie?" Megan asked.

"I'm not sure, but she asked you guys to be there at 11:00."

"We'll be there!"

As Clint arrived at work, the parking lot looked more full than usual for this early on a Saturday. There were banners and balloons and several inflatable toys for children outside the building.

"Must be some kind of special promotion," Clint thought as he pulled in. When he stepped out of his car, he saw James and Julie in the parking lot. James

was the community development director for the business. He had a really fun job: finding ways the business could add value in the community.

"Good morning," Clint said. "What's going on today?"

They looked at each other and then at Clint. James said, "It looks like we pulled it off."

"We did," Julie said.

"What did you pull off?" Clint was confused. "What did I miss?"

"The surprise," James said.

"What surprise?"

"This," Julie said as she gestured toward the parking lot. "This is for you!"

"What? Now I'm really confused."

"Not you personally. For the well."

"The well?"

"Yes, it's *Dig a Well Day*."

"It is?"

"Yes!"

"Is that a national holiday?"

"No, we made it up! We are giving some of our profits today to your project, and we're inviting our customers to contribute as well."

"How did you get the word out?"

"There's this little thing called social media, Clint. You need to get out more," Julie laughed. "Come on, we have work to do."

The day was a big hit. As it turned out, a lot of people want to make a difference in the world, and providing a well for Baako's village was a perfect opportunity.

At 11:00, Blake, Megan, and Kristin arrived just in time to hear a brief word from Julie. She stood in front of the counter to speak to the team members and customers gathered there.

"Thanks for coming today. You guys are amazing! You have supported every cause we've ever introduced to you. You have a big heart and you are all making a big difference. Your impact is far-reaching. Thank you!

"Today, we are helping Clint, Tyler, Olivia, and their friend Alex raise money to build a well for a remote village in Africa. It's a place they've all visited and a place of tremendous need. Thanks, guys, for your compassion and your vision. Based on what we've received thus far, I think you're going to build wells for a couple of villages. We've already raised about $17,000!"

Everyone clapped and there were lots of hugs. Julie said, "Thanks again for coming!" She turned to her team and said, "Back to work."

Clint went to see his mom and dad, while Tyler and Olivia went back behind the counter. Both had been hired shortly after Clint gave them the thumbs up. Even though Olivia had a broken arm at the time, Julie said, "Never pass on Top Talent." They both loved the place and, like Clint, would find a way to stay on in a part-time capacity after school started back.

Clint gave his parents a hug and said, "Thanks for coming!" He looked at the crowd, "All of this for the well."

———————

Never pass on Top Talent.

———————

"It's unbelievable!" Megan beamed.

At that moment, Julie approached the group. Clint said, "Mom, Dad, Kristin, this is Julie. Julie, this is my family."

"Proud to meet you," Julie said. "This is an amazing young man you've raised here."

"We are proud of him," Megan said.

Then Blake spoke up. "I've been looking forward to meeting you. I know today is crazy, but I would love to find time to buy you a cup of coffee."

❂ ❂ ❂

The African sun was setting over Maasai land, the dust was thick, and the crowd was huge. It was Clint's turn to speak.

"I'm thankful to be with you today—all of us are: Tyler, Alex, and Olivia, too. Baako, we feel your pain and loss. We miss Amara. However, she lives on in our hearts.

"Even though we live thousands of miles away, we want you to know you are loved. Not in an abstract way, but tangibly. This well is just one expression of that love.

"This occasion reminds me of an ancient proverb: 'The one who drinks the water should never forget the one who dug the well.'

"Amara dug this well for you. We pray you, your children, and your children's children will always remember her and drink from it in good health."

Epilogue

The well was dug and the celebration continued deep into the night; there were hugs and tears and good-byes. But it would not be the last time Clint and his friends would visit Africa. Thanks to Julie and her customers' support, plus the money Clint, Tyler, Olivia, and Alex were able to raise, they have been able to build nine wells—so far.

Julie's business continues to flourish. She had created a powerful Talent Magnet of her own. However, like Blake and so many others on this journey, she had underleveraged her creation. She had not focused on getting the word out. After she and Blake met and compared notes, her team decided to create a strategic communications plan to let people know about their business and what they had to offer. As she and Blake became friends, they shared many cups of coffee and helped each other create even stronger high-performance organizations.

Sam turned from critic to crusader. He changed the entire culture of his organization—and it started with his people. Apparently, they were holding his organization back. The turnaround began like all others: with the leader. As of this writing, several of his properties have been recognized nationally as top spots to stay.

Blake and Charles continue to enjoy an amazing partnership. Day by day, they are quietly building one of the best-run organizations on the planet. And, based on the number of applicants they now receive on an annual basis, it looks like the Talent Magnet they have created is working extremely well.

Acknowledgments

This has been one of the most challenging and fulfilling projects of my career to date. The real fun has been the hundreds of people I've interacted with and learned from along the way. I want to give a shout-out to as many as possible.

The team from Prophet—Siobhan Cooper, Ellie Thornton, Helen Rosethorn, and Mike Fleming—thanks for your passion, diligence, and professionalism from inception to final insights. Your team is phenomenal!

The AON team—Chris Adair, Rebecca Williams, Pete Sanborn, and Richmond Fourmy, thank you for helping us do ground-breaking research on an extremely aggressive timeline! The truths you helped us discover will have world-changing impact.

Thanks to the leaders from around the nation who let us take a look at your performance data and then survey your people. That took real courage! I trust the outcome of this work will serve you and your organizations for years to come.

To the leaders listed below who allowed us to interview your Top Talent . . . many of the ideas you've just read about were discovered during our visits with you. Thank you!

Billy Lynch, Bob Garrett, Bob Kyle, Brandon Hurst, Brandon LaMarque, Brian Smith, Bruce Smith, Bryan Bullington, Chuck King, Dan Curran, Daniel Grier, Daryl Saylor, Dave Terhune, Dean Sandbo, Erich Weiss, Erik DeVriendt, Glenn Rosson, Jason Ward, Jay Hawkins, Jeremy Smith, Joe Pumilia, John Roden, Jonathan Winn, Kersh Peterson, Kevin Harrison, Lauren Plain, Mark Cook, MeriBeth McNeill, Mike Holmes, Mike Ludwig, Natalie Martz, Natasha Gilbert, Paul Rankin, Philip Thomas, Quart Graves, Rob Morris, Robert Barnes, Robert Hensen, Rob Rabenecker, Rocky DeStefano, Roger Clark, Ron Trout, Rusty Wylie, Shawn York, Todd Kalish, Tony Carrico, and William Boulware.

And, thanks to the literally hundreds of Top Talent we talked to during our journey. I've tried to represent your voice well.

Jessica Hampton, Bill Dunphy, Jeff Steggert, Ryan Bowman, and Boone Smith, thanks for your work behind the scenes to add value to this project.

Donna Miller, Randy Gravitt, Justin Miller, Steve Piersanti, Laura Larson, Janice Rutledge, Ken Fracaro, Mike McNair, Sara Jane Hope, and Shay Pursel—thanks for, again, helping me communicate truth with clarity and simplicity.

Lindsay Miller, Lasell Whipple, and Peter Hobbs—I love the cover! Thanks for your creativity and your willingness to work with me. I think we make a good team.

And finally, for those who read these pages and find them helpful, thanks for sharing this book with others!

About the Author

Mark Miller is a best-selling author, business leader, and communicator.

Mark began writing almost twenty years ago when he teamed up with Ken Blanchard, coauthor of *The One Minute Manager,* to write *The Secret: What Great Leaders Know and Do.* The book you hold is his seventh. With over a million books in print, in more than twenty-five languages, Mark's global impact continues to grow.

In addition to his writing, Mark enjoys speaking to leaders. Over the years, he's traveled to dozens of countries teaching for numerous international organizations. His theme is always the same: encouraging and equipping leaders!

Mark started his Chick-fil-A career working as an hourly team member in 1977. In 1978, he joined the corporate staff working in the warehouse and mailroom. Since that time, he has provided leadership for

Corporate Communications, Field Operations, Quality and Customer Satisfaction, Training and Development, and Leadership Development. During his tenure with Chick-fil-A, the company has grown from seventy-five restaurants to over 2,300 locations with annual sales approaching $10 billion.

Mark lives an active lifestyle. As a photographer, he enjoys shooting in some of the world's hardest-to-reach places. Past locations include Antarctica, Everest Base Camp, the jungles of Rwanda, and the Galápagos Islands.

Married to Donna, his high school sweetheart, for over thirty-five years, Mark has two sons, Justin and David, a daughter-in-law, Lindsay, and two amazing grandchildren, Addie and Logan!

Mark would love to connect with you via . . .

Cell: 678-612-8441

Twitter: @LeadersServe

LinkedIn: Mark Miller

Instagram: TMarkMiller (mostly personal items)

About the Research

This project and book were born out of the question:

What attracts top talent?

Our original intent was to purchase secondary research to answer this question. I was shocked to find no such research existed; therefore, we commissioned our own. We partnered with Prophet, a global brand agency, and AON, a global leader in Human Resources, to help us throughout the journey.

During the various phases of the project, we used four independent research methods: live interviews with leaders and top talent, ethnography, a quantitative survey comparing responses from top and typical talent (samples derived from historical performance data), and a multistage panel survey.

In the end, over 7,000 people participated in the various phases. The study group included all fifty states, and personal interviews were conducted in thirty-eight cities. The combined methods reached people from age fourteen to sixty-five+ and included both professional and hourly workers across all educational backgrounds.

Mark Miller's High Performance Series

Leaders Made Here
Building a Leadership Culture

Great leaders create great organizations. However, a scarcity of leaders today means a shortfall in performance tomorrow. Don't gamble with your company's future!

Mark Miller describes how to nurture leaders throughout the organization, from the front lines to the executive ranks. *Leaders Made Here* outlines a clear and replicable approach to creating the leadership bench every organization needs.

Hardcover, 144 pages, ISBN 978-1-62656-981-2
PDF ebook, ISBN 978-1-62656-982-9
ePub ebook 978-1-62656-983-6
Digital audio 978-1-62656-985-0

Chess Not Checkers
Elevate Your Leadership Game

The early days of an organization are like checkers: a quickly played game with mostly interchangeable pieces. But as the organization expands, the same old moves won't cut it anymore. You have to think strategically, plan ahead, and leverage every employee's specific talents—that's chess. Mark Miller outlines four essential strategies that will transform your leadership and your organization!

Hardcover, 144 pages, ISBN 978-1-62656-394-0
PDF ebook, ISBN 978-1-62656-395-7
ePub ebook 978-1-62656-396-4
Digital audiobook 978-1-62656-603-3

Berrett–Koehler Publishers, Inc.
www.bkconnection.com   **800.929.2929**

Also by Mark Miller

The Heart of Leadership
Becoming a Leader People Want to Follow

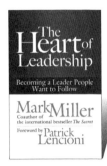

In this enlightening and entertaining business fable, Mark Miller identifies the five unique character traits exhibited by exceptional leaders. When Blake Brown is passed over for a promotion, he is sent on a quest to meet with five of his late father's colleagues, each of whom holds a piece of the leadership puzzle. This book shows us that leadership needn't be the purview of the few—it is within reach for millions around the world.

Hardcover, 144 pages, ISBN 978-1-60994-960-0
PDF ebook, ISBN 978-1-60994-961-7
ePub ebook ISBN 978-1-60994-962-4

The Secret of Teams
What Great Teams Know and Do

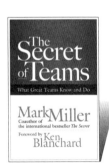

What separates teams that really deliver from the ones that simply spin their wheels? In this book, executive Debbie Brewster learns from three very different teams— the Special Forces, NASCAR, and a local restaurant. Debbie and her team discover the three elements that all high-performing teams have in common, how to change entrenched ways of thinking and acting, how to measure your progress, and more.

Hardcover, 144 pages, ISBN 978-1-60994-093-5
PDF ebook, ISBN 978-1-60994-109-3
ePub ebook 978-1-60994-110-9

Berrett–Koehler Publishers, Inc.
www.bkconnection.com   800.929.2929

With Ken Blanchard

The Secret
What Great Leaders Know and Do, Third Edition

Join struggling young executive Debbie Brewster as she explores a profound yet seemingly contradictory concept: to lead is to serve. Along the way she learns why great leaders seem preoccupied with the future, what three arenas require continuous improvement, the two essential components to leadership success, how to knowingly strengthen—or unwittingly destroy—leadership credibility, and more.

Hardcover, 144 pages, ISBN 978-1-62656-198-4
PDF ebook, ISBN 978-1-62656-199-1
ePub ebook ISBN 978-1-62656-200-4

Great Leaders Grow
Becoming a Leader for Life

What is the key ingredient for a long-term, high-impact career in leadership? Debbie Brewster tells Blake Brown, her late mentor's son, "Your capacity to grow determines your capacity to lead" and helps Blake discover and apply four strategies for personal growth. These same strategies can enhance your life and leadership too! Join Blake and explore the path to increased leadership effectiveness and influence.

Hardcover, 144 pages, ISBN 978-1-60994-303-5
PDF ebook, ISBN 978-1-60509-695-7
ePub ebook, ISBN 978-1-60509-696-4

Berrett–Koehler Publishers, Inc.
www.bkconnection.com   **800.929.2929**

Berrett–Koehler
Publishers

Berrett-Koehler is an independent publisher dedicated to an ambitious mission: *Connecting people and ideas to create a world that works for all.*

We believe that the solutions to the world's problems will come from all of us, working at all levels: in our organizations, in our society, and in our own lives. Our BK Business books help people make their organizations more humane, democratic, diverse, and effective (we don't think there's any contradiction there). Our BK Currents books offer pathways to creating a more just, equitable, and sustainable society. Our BK Life books help people create positive change in their lives and align their personal practices with their aspirations for a better world.

All of our books are designed to bring people seeking positive change together around the ideas that empower them to see and shape the world in a new way.

And we strive to practice what we preach. At the core of our approach is Stewardship, a deep sense of responsibility to administer the company for the benefit of all of our stakeholder groups including authors, customers, employees, investors, service providers, and the communities and environment around us. Everything we do is built around this and our other key values of quality, partnership, inclusion, and sustainability.

This is why we are both a B-Corporation and a California Benefit Corporation—a certification and a for-profit legal status that require us to adhere to the highest standards for corporate, social, and environmental performance.

We are grateful to our readers, authors, and other friends of the company who consider themselves to be part of the BK Community. We hope that you, too, will join us in our mission.

A BK Business Book

We hope you enjoy this BK Business book. BK Business books pioneer new leadership and management practices and socially responsible approaches to business. They are designed to provide you with groundbreaking and practical tools to transform your work and organizations while upholding the triple bottom line of people, planet, and profits. High-five!

To find out more, visit **www.bkconnection.com**.

Berrett–Koehler
Publishers

Connecting people and ideas
to create a world that works for all

Dear Reader,

Thank you for picking up this book and joining our worldwide community of Berrett-Koehler readers. We share ideas that bring positive change into people's lives, organizations, and society.

To welcome you, we'd like to offer you a free e-book. You can pick from among twelve of our bestselling books by entering the promotional code **BKP92E** here: http://www.bkconnection.com/welcome.

When you claim your free e-book, we'll also send you a copy of our e-newsletter, the *BK Communiqué*. Although you're free to unsubscribe, there are many benefits to sticking around. In every issue of our newsletter you'll find

- A free e-book
- Tips from famous authors
- Discounts on spotlight titles
- Hilarious insider publishing news
- A chance to win a prize for answering a riddle

Best of all, our readers tell us, "Your newsletter is the only one I actually read." So claim your gift today, and please stay in touch!

Sincerely,

Charlotte Ashlock
Steward of the BK Website

Questions? Comments? Contact me at bkcommunity@bkpub.com.